High School

High School

David Owen

The Viking Press New York

First published in 1981 by The Viking Press
625 Madison Avenue, New York, N.Y. 10022
Published simultaneously in Canada by
Penguin Books Canada Limited

LIBRARY OF CONGRESS CATALOGING IN PUBLICATION DATA
Owen, David, 1955–
High school
1. High schools. I. Title.
LB1607.O94   373.73   80–54079
ISBN 0–670–37149–1

A portion of this book appeared originally in *Esquire* in different form.

Grateful acknowledgment is made to the following for permission to reprint copyrighted material:

Alfred A. Knopf, Inc.: A selection from "In Football Season" from *The Music School* by John Updike. Copyright © 1962 by John Updike.

Macmillan Publishing Co., Inc., and A. P. Watt Ltd.: A selection from "Sailing to Byzantium" from *Collected Poems* by William Butler Yeats. Copyright 1928 by Macmillan Publishing Co., Inc., renewed 1956 by Georgie Yeats.

Printed in the United States of America
Set in Linotron Century Schoolbook

For the real high school students in my family:

John Owen, '81
Ned Hodgman, '82
Cornelia Hodgman, '80

Contents

Preface   ix

Part One: September   1

    1. Orientation   3
    2. "Put On Your Hats!"   16
    3. Cheetos   31
    4. P.E.   42
    5. Getting High   53
    6. Progress   59
    7. Real Progress   67

Part Two: October   83

    8. Burning Goobers   85
    9. Journalism   94
   10. Futures   108
   11. "Them Little Numbers"   122
   12. Girls   130
   13. Dancing   138
   14. "A Boat of Nowhere"   147

Part Three: November   163

    15. True Love   165
    16. "A Witness to History"   175
    17. "Stinks and Boring"   189
    18. Fearful Symmetry   200
    19. Grades   209
    20. Eisenhower 10, Bingham 0   217

Part Four: December   233

    21. Par-*tee*   235
    22. The Shit Hits the Fan   246
    23. Leaving   253

Afterword: My Class   258

Author's Note   263

❧ Preface

The past is a foreign country; they do things
differently there.

—L. P. Hartley

All that anyone with a high school diary has to do to
make himself feel humble is to reread a few of the old entries. I
am appalled when I look back at the abortive journals I began in
the aftermaths of romantic crises when I was sixteen and
seventeen years old. No one could have been so naïve. Yet there
it all is, on paper, and in my handwriting: "I am not saying it
was all bullshit. For a while I think she had conquered her
un-feeling-ness (for lack of a better word) and was really
feeling." Feeling. The word reverberated through my adolescence. "The vast majority of them [i.e., certain girls] seem to be
incapable of showing or feeling any true emotions"; "I want to
write down what I am feeling but I don't know where to start";
"After the Hot Tuna concert, C—— and I came back here. She
let me read a diary that she is keeping which nobody has ever
seen. It was amazing—I have felt every feeling that she wrote

down in there. Most of the time, you think you're the only person in the world who feels the way you do."

Compared with the dazzling newness of so many teenage experiences, the world of adults seems positively banal. Grownups still talk, sometimes endlessly, about their feelings, but after the age of twenty-one or so, the word begins to take on a different meaning. When an adult says "I feel" he usually means nothing more urgent than "I think." Thank God. But something powerful is lost when the brain reasserts its predominance over the ductless glands.

It was partly in order to see if I could rediscover something of the old hormonal intensity of adolescence that I decided toward the end of my twenty-fourth year to enroll in a high school as a seventeen-year-old member of the graduating class of 1980. Rereading my old journals, I had begun to wonder about the connections between a teenager and the adult he or she eventually becomes. I wanted to experience high school again from the vantage point of an adult, to check my old impressions against a set of new ones. I also wanted simply to find out what teenagers are up to these days. Adolescents are not in the news so much as they were when I was in school and during the decade prior to my graduation. I wanted to see how today's teenagers compare with those of ten years ago, and to find out what has changed and what has remained the same in a typical American high school experience.

I entered high school in 1969 and graduated in 1973. My original experience is thus roughly a decade old. That is not very old. It can be argued that members of the class of 1980 and I belong to the same generation. But a lot has happened in the last ten years. On the day I graduated from high school, the Watergate tapes were undiscovered, American soldiers were still in Vietnam, the speed limit on I-70 in Kansas was seventy-five miles an hour, and it was possible to buy gasoline on the outskirts of Kansas City, my hometown, for less than thirty cents a gallon. While the changes of the last decade have touched everyone in our society, in some ways they have been felt—or will be felt—most intensely by the young. It was in order to find out how they are bearing up that I decided to go back.

My plan, as it was finally worked out with the help of editors and friends, particularly my wife, was to enter a public high school on the first day of the school year and leave it approximately four months later at the end of the first semester. The school I chose was a relatively large one in a middle-sized town roughly two hours from New York. Statistically, at least, both the school and the town were "typical." By the time I left them, I hoped, I would have been assimilated into the life of the school and would be able to describe its workings not as an observer but as a participant. I would enroll as a bona fide senior and take every precaution not to be found out. I wanted to feel what the other students were feeling and to think of our fortunes as rising and falling on the same tide. And that, more or less, is what I did.

I am especially grateful to my wife, Ann Hodgman, who made many improvements in the manuscript and remained surprisingly calm during the four months she was married to a seventeen-year-old; to my agent, Julia Stevenson, who performed nobly as a critic, adviser, and "mother"; to my editor, Vicky Stein, who in addition to sound editorial advice supplied me with vivid recollections of her own high school experiences; to Richard and Eileen Giarniero, who showed me great kindness and who were indispensable in helping me preserve my cover; to my mother, father, sister, and brother, who have an unnerving recall of all the embarrassing things I did when I was in high school; to all my in-laws, three of whom either go to high school or teach it; to Betsy Carter, senior editor at *Esquire* magazine, who helped determine the final form of this book; and to scores of students, teachers, and administrators who made my life infinitely more interesting and whom I will never be able to thank in person.

Part One

 September

Adolescent doubts are very tedious to the mature.

—Evelyn Waugh

1
⟫Orientation

It was 10:30 in the morning, half an hour after my appointment with a Bingham High School guidance counselor had been scheduled to begin. I was sitting in an old and uncomfortable wooden chair and worrying that when I finally had to open my mouth I would be too nervous to speak. With me was my agent, Julia Stevenson, who was posing as my mother. She was wearing a grim black dress and an ornate wedding band for which she had paid a dollar in a junk shop on West 14th Street in New York. The dress, she said, was the only article of clothing she owned that looked even vaguely "maternal." (Several weeks before, my real mother had asked, a little anxiously, "So what's this woman like, anyway?") I was wearing a brand-new pair of wire-rimmed aviator glasses, a blue-white-and-yellow shirt I hadn't worn since tenth grade, blue jeans, Toob Sox, and a hastily purchased pair of Korean-made running shoes. Julia leaned over, smiled craftily, and whispered, "Get your hair out of your eyes. And tuck in your shirt."

A few days before, Julia and I had met in a Third Avenue bar to practice our routine. When the waitress brought our drinks

Julia looked me up and down and said, "Quit slouching." I sat up immediately. Julia grinned evilly.

Now, in the Guidance Office, we were exchanging nervous glances and trying to keep track of the several dozen fabricated details that added up to our fictional identities: We had just moved to Bingham from Kansas City, Missouri, where Julia's husband, my father, had unexpectedly lost his job as an advertising copywriter; we had moved East in the hope of giving Dad a fresh start—poor old Dad, he just wasn't much of a provider; we had chosen Bingham because of its modest cost of living and its relative proximity to New York. In her purse Julia had several documents that I had laboriously forged over the preceding weeks. There was a counterfeit report card from the school I had supposedly attended in Kansas City, and a document verifying that I had received all my vaccinations. There was also a bogus birth certificate showing me to be seventeen years old. Finally, there was a standard apartment lease, which I had filled out for an obscure address in the Bingham school district, to establish our residency. (As it turned out, we needed neither the birth certificate nor the lease.)

The guidance counselor, meanwhile, was arranging some papers on the windowsill behind her desk. She was not at all as I had imagined her. An officious voice I had heard on the telephone at the end of the summer, when I called to find out when the school year began, had led me to expect a severe woman of eighty or ninety who would look me in the eye for a few painful seconds and then call the police. Instead, here was a small, middle-aged woman with a thoroughly disarming face, gigantic round glasses, and a slightly batty smile. From time to time she turned from the windowsill to snatch a document from the chaos of her desk. Each time she turned, she smiled at me.

At last she introduced herself. Her name, she said, was Mrs. Wheelock. She had been a guidance counselor at Bingham High for many years, but this term she had been given double duties: Two days a week she would be fulfilling a similar function at

Eisenhower High School, Bingham High's newer, more affluent
sister on the other side of town. This would require her to keep
two separate sets of files and to transport them from one school
to the other in the back of her car. She said she only hoped she
would be able to keep everybody straight.

I hoped she wouldn't. While her back was turned I craned my
neck to read the papers on her desk, looking for a clue as to what
might happen next. The only thing I could read clearly was the
name typed on the label of a large manila folder: OWEN, David.
The sight of my name in that sea of forms was distinctly
unsettling. I gulped and tried to remember my story.

"Well, David," Mrs. Wheelock said, "we're happy to have you
with us." She sat so lightly in her chair she could have been
hovering above it. Her smile was entrancing. She reached into
an open drawer and handed me a mimeographed sheet, a map of
the school, and a little purple book. At the top of the mimeographed sheet was my homeroom assignment: B-11. The purple
booklet was a guide to the rules and traditions of the school. My
copy opened to "Hail, Bingham!":

> Bingham, sing thy praises of glory
> Filled with honor and loyalty
> O'er hill and dale.
> Bingham, ring forever the rally
> Of the thundering victories
> Of thy dear name.
> Time n'er will plunder
> The memories we hold.
> Oh! Alma Mater
> Oh! Purple and Gold.
> Hail! Bingham, Alma Mater of mothers
> Wave thy banner forever
> Oh! Bingham High

As I tried to conceive of a melody to contain these lines, the
absurdity of the entire project struck me. How was it possible

that Mrs. Wheelock had failed to realize that Julia and I were imposters? Any minute now, the three of us would burst into laughter, admit that it had all been a good joke, and go our separate ways.

But the interview went on, for nearly an hour. After determining my level of achievement, we selected appropriate courses. I had given myself C's and B's on my phony report card, hoping those marks would place me close to the mean, but they put me near the middle of the top half of the class. After some animated discussion we decided to enroll me in World Literature, a comprehensive English course for seniors; Math B, a slightly accelerated elaboration of Algebra II; American History Since World War I, a required course; Accounting I, "to please your father," Julia said, masterfully; and Foundations of Psychology. This last seemed just the thing. Bingham High School's course catalog described it as "A study of human behavior designed to enlarge the student's awareness of himself and others."

By the time we were midway through course selection, Julia had to remind me with a stern glance that Physics and French IV, two courses I had said I wanted to take, might not leave even an ambitious twelfth grader enough free time to write a book. I was beginning ever so slightly to resent this parental authority figure sitting at my side. I was also beginning to feel just a little bit bored. A meeting with a guidance counselor is, let's face it, a tedious piece of business. You have to sit up straight and be all ears while your mother speaks realistically about your aptitudes to a total stranger. Even though I was perfectly aware that Julia wasn't really my mother, I bridled a little when she said she didn't think I would be able to handle the math course I was signed up for.

As the meeting dragged on, I began to worry less and less about whether we would pull it off and more and more about whether I would fit in at Bingham. Would I ever make any friends? That question hadn't been given too much consideration in our recent strategy conferences. Now I looked out the window at some students in the courtyard, my classmates-to-be, and my first thought was, "Jesus, they all look about twenty years old."

Mrs. Wheelock moved on to the subject of extracurricular activities. "Do you think you would have any interest in going out for one of the teams?" she asked. I said I doubted it. Julia said I had been thinking about going out for basketball, hadn't I? I looked down and said maybe.

"How tall are you?" Mrs. Wheelock asked.

"Six foot two."

Julia looked at me with pride. "Can you believe it?" she said. She reached over and ruffled my hair affectionately. I managed to blush.

Mrs. Wheelock turned pale.

"We don't do that anymore!" she gasped, giving Julia an angry glance. Mrs. Wheelock was genuinely upset. Apparently the American mother's license to embarrass her children with public displays of affection had been rescinded, at least in the Bingham Guidance Office. I was glad to hear it. Mrs. Wheelock smiled a little nervously in my direction. I realized that throughout our interview she had focused her attention almost exclusively on me, and not on the woman she took to be my mother. When we were weighing the merits of different courses, she asked me which ones I thought I would enjoy. When Julia brought up college, Mrs. Wheelock turned to me to ask what my interests were and what I wanted to do with my life (I said I didn't know). When I decided definitely that I wanted to take a particular course, she would say, "Yes, I was leaning in that direction myself," or, "That's just what I was thinking." Whatever else they have done, the "sensitivity" movements that gathered steam in the United States in the 1970s have softened the hearts of high school guidance counselors. I thumbed through my purple booklet and read a paragraph labeled "Dress Philosophy":

A dress code, while not overly restrictive and out-of-step, should be a kind of unwritten understanding that immoderate or inappropriate "stand outs" in dress are not allowed. Your best guide in a question such as this, which involves so much personal taste, is the common sense to know what is attractive individually, or what is selfishly disrespectful of another student's real reason for being at Bingham High.

The buttery rhetoric of conciliation. That's what my old classmates and I used to long for in our ideological wars of attrition with high school administrators. We would have died to hear a school official utter the words "unwritten understanding." When I was in eleventh grade, the principal detained all of us after assembly one morning and ordered the boys to march past him single file. If anyone's hair extended below his collar, he was given the choice of going immediately to the barber or having his locks shorn right there, by the principal, with a heavy pair of black-handled utility scissors. I climbed out through one of the windows with several of my friends.

The winds of change in secondary education sometimes blow in conflicting directions. At my old high school, while the principal was insisting on archaically restrictive codes for hair and dress, the English department was busy jettisoning anything that smelled even remotely of the past. Shakespeare was still represented, feebly, by the handful of plays that seem to exist only in high school curricula—plays like *The Taming of the Shrew* and *Two Gentlemen of Verona*—but in most other quarters the only important century was held to be the twentieth. In various English classes I read the novels of Kurt Vonnegut, a biography of Al Capone, Richard Brautigan's poetry, and *A Clockwork Orange*. Ernest Hemingway was accorded respect usually reserved for Virgil. In tenth-grade English we spent six weeks "making something" with our hands.

The Bingham course catalog, I was interested to see, described World Literature this way: "The early development of western literature, especially drama and poetry, is studied in readings from the Anglo-Saxons, Chaucer, Shakespeare, Milton, and other writers, mainly British, through the eighteenth century. A high level of critical writing and of student participation in class is expected." I have been around long enough not to be seduced by course descriptions, but even so, the general emphasis seemed admirable.

When we left the Guidance Office Julia asked me if I wanted to take a look around. The only students now at school were the sophomores, who were being given the opportunity to get used to their new surroundings without the distracting presence of upperclassmen.

Julia and I started in what seemed to be a promising direction. The wide hallway before us was immaculate. The floor had been buffed to a high gloss over the summer, and its reflective surface had not yet been dulled by armies of dragging feet. Everything was suffused with that numbing light found only in high schools, hospitals, and craters on the moon. The lighting fixtures hummed. I was immediately and vividly conscious of my face. Fluorescent light seems to leave a coating on the skin. Irony of ironies, no pimple is more visible than a pimple in a high school.

We passed an open doorway. A girl was standing just inside, staring at us, and as we walked past she asked if we were lost. An accompanying mother, I suddenly realized, is an international teenage signal of distress. I might as well have rolled by in a wheelchair. Quickly I looked for avenues of escape. As we turned away a bell rang piercingly just above my head. Doors at the end of the hallway opened and thirty or forty sophomores came surging toward us.

"Come on," I said to Julia, hoping to spare myself a kind of embarrassment I wasn't sure she would understand, "let's get out of here."

Bingham High School looks exactly like what it is. The bricks in its façade were pressed from the same somber yellow mud used in high school buildings all across the country. Three towering maple trees shade the narrow yard in front of the building and in autumn cover the sidewalks with yellow and orange leaves—like a picture on the cover of any yearbook. Viewed from directly in front of the main entrance, the building looks the same as it must have for the last fifty years. The only anachronism is the New Wing, added in the early 1960s, off to the left. Like the main part of the building, the New Wing is made of yellow bricks, but its lines are sleeker and more severe. In 1964 the bronze dedicatory plaque near the entrance to the New Wing was wrenched from the bricks and a new one, inscribed IN MEMORIAM, JOHN FITZGERALD KENNEDY, was put in its place. There's been no new construction at Bingham since then. Camelot is over; the baby boom has come and gone.

Bingham High School was built in 1922 on a few acres of ground bequeathed to the town by one of its nineteenth-century benefactors. It replaced the struggling Town School, which had occupied half a dozen temporary sites over the previous forty years. In 1958, as the first war babies were reaching adolescence, a second high school, Dwight D. Eisenhower, was added a couple of miles away. Bingham and Eisenhower are bitter and perpetual rivals, the competition intensified by the fact that there are distinct differences between the two school districts. Whereas Eisenhower families tend to be upwardly mobile and fairly recently arrived, Bingham families are solidly working class and lower middle class, many of them with strong roots in the community. The fast-food franchises and Laundromats that line the main drag in the Bingham end of town gradually give way to real-estate offices and drive-in banks designed to look like houses—flat little colonial numbers with shutters on the windows and sprinklers in the yards—at the Eisenhower end. There are a handful of landmark buildings near the center of town, but these gradually fade into gas pumps and plate glass and aluminum siding toward Bingham. Farther down the road, out past the edge of town, are the half-dozen major factories that employ a large proportion of the Bingham work force.

The Bingham High School district is, in other words, an "average" community. Its median family income approximates the national average, as does Bingham High School's black/white mix, its percentage of college-bound seniors, and its general levels of achievement. Bingham High School's student population, which covers grades ten through twelve, is about 1300; 250 of the kids are black. To the extent that such statistics are meaningful, Bingham High School is a typical American school.

When I arrived in Bingham for my first day of school, the sky was perfectly blue. The air was warm but there was a hint of autumn crispness in the breeze. I was dressed as I had been for my meeting with the guidance counselor the week before, with the addition of a mangy green crew-neck sweater: it had been cold in Manhattan at five o'clock that morning when I set out for school. I was carrying a blue three-ring binder filled with wide-lined notebook paper and half a dozen flimsy subject dividers, all of which I had bought in a grocery store on Saturday. I approached the school from across the street, and paused for several minutes to size it up before finding the nerve to go inside.

It was still early, but six or seven boys were gathered on the front steps, smoking cigarettes. I dreaded having to pass them.

From fifty yards away they looked about as friendly and forgiving as checkpoint guards. But there was no alternative. I made a dash through the morning traffic, climbed the steps as coolly and calmly as I could, and pulled hard on the handle of the door on the left, which was locked. The boys smoked and stared. I reached for the other door, tripped over the last step, and stumbled inside.

Mrs. Wheelock had told me on Friday to report first thing to the Guidance Office, so I checked in there. The office was crowded with new students, most of whom were milling around nervously in silence. Harried counselors strode back and forth carrying clipboards crammed with papers. Mrs. Wheelock spotted me almost immediately and took me aside. "Are you nervous?" she asked.

"A little," I said.

"Well, don't you worry about a thing." She collared a boy standing several feet away. "This is George Menaro. He's in your homeroom. George, this is David Owen. He came all the way from Kansas City. You take him with you and introduce him to Mr. Amberson and see that he gets to his first class. Mr. Amberson, David, will give you your schedule."

George looked pained. "All right," he said finally. "But first I gotta go to my locker." He was out the door and halfway down the hall before I could thank Mrs. Wheelock. I jogged after him and followed him up the stairs.

George was of average height and had longish curly brown hair and a pair of aviator glasses almost identical to mine. He was wearing Pro-Keds, white corduroy jeans, and a black T-shirt that said LED ZEPPELIN on the front. He opened his locker and took out a spiral notebook.

"You new?" he asked, bewilderingly.

I said yes and tried to think of something friendly and appropriate to add, but George was already off again down the hall. He stopped to talk to someone he knew, a short boy in an oversized letter jacket. I hung back, expecting to be introduced. I wasn't. George took off again. This time I was right behind him. He stopped at a door labeled B-11 and went inside. There were three other students already in the room. Mr. Amberson was not there.

George put down his notebook on a desk in the first row and went over to talk to one of the other students. I wondered if I should follow him, then decided against it. From the way he turned his back when he sat down it was clear he believed his small responsibility for me had ended. Through the window I could see several yellow school buses pulling up in front of the building and discharging their passengers. All the students on one of the buses were black, all the students on another were white. I stood awkwardly at the front of the room and tried to drop my notebook casually on the desk next to George's. Then Mr. Amberson walked in.

He hoisted a big formed-plastic briefcase to the top of his desk and smiled.

"I'm a new student," I said quietly. "My name is David Owen."

"Ah, yes, David Owen. Where ya from, Dave?"

"Kansas City."

"Not bad! Missouri or Kansas?"

"Missouri."

"Not bad!"

He gave me a handful of cards to fill out and told me that I could sit wherever I wanted, but the seat I chose would be mine for the rest of the year. I asked him if he had my schedule.

"Schedule?" he said. "No, I don't think so." He flipped through a stack of papers on his desk. "No, sorry, Dave, I don't see a schedule. You'll have to go down to Guidance for that. Just leave all those cards here, and you can fill them out later."

I went back down to the Guidance Office. The general crush had tamed itself into a long line at the receptionist's desk. Mrs. Wheelock was nowhere to be seen. I slipped in at the end of the line and, five or ten minutes later, explained my problem to the receptionist. She said that if my homeroom teacher hadn't had my schedule before, then he would surely have it by now. I went back to B-11, but Mr. Amberson hadn't heard anything new. He suggested I go back to Guidance. This time Mrs. Wheelock was there; she told me to go to the principal's office.

"What's the problem?" a secretary in the principal's office asked me.

"I need a schedule."

"Did you lose yours?"

"No, I haven't been given one yet."

"Are you a new student?"

"Yes."

"Then your homeroom teacher will have it."

"He doesn't."

"Then you should go to Guidance."

"I did. They told me to come here."

"Well . . . all right." She pulled a folder from a huge bank of files and typed a dozen lines on a blue-and-white card. "Do you have a locker?" she asked.

"No."

She shook her head, went back to the file, and typed up another card. Then she read me some instructions from a printed sheet, looking up after every phrase to make sure her words were sinking in: "Turn the dial to the right, two or more revolutions, and stop on the first number. Turn the dial to the left, one revolution (past the first number once) and keep turning the dial to the left," and so on. She handed me another sheet of paper, along with my schedule and combination, and sent me off to see if I could get my locker open. "If you can't do it," she said, "find a custodian and have him help you." The new sheet of paper repeated the instructions she had just read me, and added a dozen other items: "Please do not slam your locker door . . . . Your locker is not a safe . . . . Your locker will be inspected frequently by the office."

I found my locker, opened the door on the first try, and went back to B-11. The instant my hand touched the doorknob, the

bell rang. Two dozen students who did not yet know that I was
their homeroom-mate rumbled past me. George Menaro hurried
by without a hint of recognition. I stood aside and held the door.
When they had all gone I asked Mr. Amberson if he would like
me to fill out those cards now. He told me to forget about the
cards for the time being and run along to my first class.

My first class. I looked at my schedule. The first line said: 12
1 MTWRF R23 PSYCH L CHAPIN. Translation: Semesters 1 and 2,
first period, Monday through Friday (the R stands for Thursday), psychology in Room R-23 with someone named L. Chapin.
I studied my map for a minute or two and then set out to find
Room R-23.

2

"Put On Your Hats!"

Louie Chapin, in addition to being an instructor in psychology, is the coach of Bingham High School's baseball team. Sometimes, before the first-period bell rings, he stands at the head of his psychology class and assumes the batting stance that was his trademark forty years ago in the backwaters of American baseball. He plants his big right foot and hoists an imaginary bat up high around the level of his ears. He watches for his pitch. Dawn Lavin, a pretty senior with discreet orthodontia, walks through the door with her books held tightly against her chest. The Coach's arms uncoil. "Whammo!" he cries at the midpoint of his swing. "It's outta here!" Dawn Lavin jumps a foot in the air and almost drops her books. Coach Chapin cackles behind his desk. Even after forty years, the Coach's swing is still his trademark, like Johnny Carson's famous chip shot at the beginning of the *Tonight Show*.

On the first day of school, however, the Coach's baseball history is still concealed. The most notable thing about him
this morning is the way he is dressed: a short-sleeved, loose-
knit polyester sport shirt with a thin red band around the edges
of the sleeves and collar; a wide white belt with an elliptical
buckle; voluminous casual slacks the color of the trim on his
shirt; white shoes. Like high school coaches everywhere, he is perfectly color-coordinated. His outfit looks like a vestigial athletic
uniform. I am almost surprised, when he turns around to pick
up a stack of textbooks, that there is no number on his back.

"These books still got a lot of mileage in 'em," the Coach tells
us as he hands them around. The book I receive is a 1964
revision of a work originally published in 1945. The spaces on
the stamped identification plate inside the front cover—where a
student writes his name, his homeroom number, his year of
graduation, and the condition of his book upon receipt—were all
filled in by 1973. Five more students have signed in as carefully
as possible below the plate. I add my name to the list and
appraise the book's condition, as every one of my fifteen
predecessors has, as "Excellent."

While the Coach outlines his plans for the course, I, like most
of the rest of my classmates, flip through the pages of my book. I
don't know enough about psychology to be aware of the changes
that have taken place in that field since 1964, but the book
seems a bit out of date. In a photograph on page 188, a boy who
looks strikingly like Wally in the last years of *Leave It to Beaver*
is playing a guitar in accompaniment to two admiring girls,
who are singing. Folk songs, probably. The caption says, "The
person who, like this guitarist, can contribute to the enjoyment
of others is always appreciated." A few pages farther along, a
boldface subhead asks the question, "What qualities are important in military leadership?" The answer: "During World War II
a number of interesting studies were made in an attempt to find
out what kind of men made the best military leaders. As was to

be expected, it was found that there was no 'officer type.' Modern warfare is very complex and requires leadership in many fields." Even now, a few wars later, I suppose that is probably true. I turn to a section in the middle of the book that deals with "the effects of external factors on behavior." These factors, according to the succeeding paragraph headings, are Air Circulation, Temperature, Humidity, Alcohol, Caffeine, Tobacco, and Sleep.

As I skim through my book I keep expecting to hear the chortles of my classmates. But no one makes a sound. Everyone, apparently, is taking this all in stride. Can it be that no one realizes this book would probably be of more interest to a historian than a psychologist? Or is everyone simply so cynical about school that the antiquity of the book doesn't matter? It's too early to tell. I open my book at random: "Just because one sex may tend to dominate in many situations does not mean that one sex is deriving more satisfaction from life than is another sex. As an individual learns to play his or her expected role he or she may derive a great deal of satisfaction and happiness from so doing. The individual who feels that he must fight his or her role is likely to experience a great deal of dissatisfaction and unhappiness."

The Coach pulls back the sliding door of a long storage closet that runs the length of the room. As he stows his surplus texts, I turn to the index of my book, where I can find no entries under the following terms: Birth Control, Drugs, Marijuana, Pregnancy, Rebellion, Runaways, Sex. The closest thing I can find to a mention of altered states of consciousness in teenagers is a long section on "Daydreaming" early in the book: "Sometimes individuals become concerned over their daydreams. They may even fear that daydreams indicate that they are becoming mentally ill. Such fears are unwarranted." Daydreams, the LSD of the Wally generation.

My own revery ends when the Coach begins to speak, anticipating an objection that no one has made: "There may be some different views in certain areas now than the ones that are in this book," he says, "but the basic parts are all the same. That stuff never changes. And that's what we'll be studying—the *foundations* of psychology. Some of the early stuff is pretty elementary, but when we get to Chapter Twelve on up, it gets a little more exciting. That's when it gets to people with epilepsy, that sort of thing."

Coach Chapin's classroom is Room R-23 in the New Wing of the high school building. In it he teaches not only Foundations of Psychology but also a handful of other social science electives. The room's most prominent feature, apart from the gloomy beige of the linoleum floor and the cheerful yellow of the cinderblock walls, is a green blackboard, divided into three sections, that covers most of the wall behind the Coach's desk. Just above the blackboard is a narrow panel of artificial cork that runs all the way from the window to the opposite wall. Many years ago, Coach Chapin covered the panel with rectangles of purple construction paper. The pieces nearest the window have been bleached a pale lavender by prolonged exposure to the sun. Stapled to the paper at intervals of several feet are half a dozen inspirational sayings printed on pieces of yellowed cardboard:

"To be prepared for war is one of the most effective means of preserving peace."

G. WASHINGTON

"Injustice is relatively easy to bear; what stings is justice."

H. L. MENCKEN

"Delay is preferable to error."

T. JEFFERSON

"God helps those that help themselves."

B. FRANKLIN

"Winning isn't the most important thing; it's the only thing."

V. LOMBARDI

"Those who do not remember history are condemned to repeat it."

WALTER DUNBAR

On this last card Walter Dunbar's name has been crossed out and "Georges Santanaye" has been written beside it. In the Coach's spelling, the American philosopher's Spanish name has an interesting French flavor that seems to add a new level of significance to the quotation.

There isn't much to do today, so Coach Chapin is in a jolly mood. He holds up a framed black-and-white photograph of himself and explains that it was taken a few months after the New Wing was dedicated, fifteen years ago. The picture shows him standing in front of the blackboard, the chain of inspirational sayings forming the upper margin of the image, like a pious inscription in a medieval triptych. The Coach's hair is thinner today than it was when the picture was taken, and his belly is more pronounced, but otherwise he looks about the same. In fact, if it had not occurred to him to write the day's date on the blackboard just before the photographer snapped his picture, you might not guess that the photograph is as old as it is. The date on the board is November 21, 1963. As the Coach holds up the picture for our admiration, he says, "Everybody knows what they were doing when they heard that Kennedy was shot, but how many know what they were doing the day before?"

The Coach leans back and smiles. Those of my classmates who have bothered to look up from their textbooks are perfectly stonyfaced. I realize what the matter is about the same time the Coach does. Of the thirty or so of us present today, I am the only one who can remember the Kennedy assassination, or anything else that happened in 1963. At that unforgettable moment, when the world learned that the American president had been killed—about the same time as the editors of our textbook were putting the final touches on their 1964 edition—a fair proportion of Coach Chapin's students had not yet been born. A girl sitting near me finally asks, "Which Kennedy is that, the president or the uncle?" As the Coach hastens to explain, it is impossible not to think of poor old Georges Santanaye. But then the bell rings and my first hour as a high school student is over.

Second period, according to a public-address announcement, had been preempted for seniors by something called a "Senior Hat Assembly," to be held in the auditorium. Seniors were instructed to sit in seats assigned to us in homeroom, which I had missed. When I got to the auditorium I couldn't find Mr. Amberson or any of the faces I remembered dimly from B-11. I stood at the end of one of the aisles and scanned the rows. Finally I spotted George Menaro sitting with three friends in an otherwise empty row about halfway up one side of the room. I didn't want to make a nuisance of myself again, but the assembly was about to begin. I slid into George's row and sat in the seat next to his.

"Hi," he said, surprisingly.

"I wasn't in homeroom this morning," I said, "so I didn't know where our section was."

"This ain't it."

The boy sitting next to him pointed over his shoulder. "We're supposed to be over there," he said, "but I ain't gonna sit with them assholes."

In that case, neither was I. I stowed my notebook on the floor and settled back in my seat. On the stage a fat boy was trying to attach a goosenecked microphone to a wooden lectern. When he got it hooked properly, he clicked it on and said the word "testing," loudly, ten or eleven times. Someone booed. To the right of the lectern were four seated students, the boys in three-piece suits, the girls in dresses. To the left were four seated adults. At the foot of the stage on the adult side were ten or fifteen foot-high stacks of purple sailor hats with the brims turned down. In front of each stack was a piece of cardboard with a homeroom number written on it in purple crayon.

"Fuck this shit," George said.

"What *is* a senior hat, anyway?" I asked.

George shrugged. "Just a piece of shit," he said.

"Like everything else in this fucking shithole," one of his friends added.

"I ought to ditch this fucking assembly," George said, but he stayed put.

The first speaker was Luke D'Amato, president of the senior class. He was tall and athletic-looking and wore a loosely knotted tie decorated with large overlapping disks of nonprimary colors. As he spoke he leaned one elbow on the lectern and stuck one leg out to the side. He was not a comfortable speaker. When he stumbled over one of the phrases he was reading from a stack of note cards, he shifted his weight to the other elbow and stuck his other leg out to the side.

"It gives me great pleasure," he said, after a long and rambling paean to the potential of the senior class, "to introduce you to your principal for this year, a man with whom I have not yet had the pleasure of working with yet, Mr. Shenck."

Principal Shenck was ominously tall and had a grim crop of short black hair. He looked about forty-five. He was wearing black-and-white checked pants, a bright blue blazer, a blue shirt, and a brown tie. This was his first year as principal, I knew. He had been promoted from assistant principal over the summer when his predecessor had accepted an appointment somewhere else.

Mr. Shenck was greeted with a huge burst of applause,

though not from my row. The main body of his supporters seemed to be a fair-sized group of well-dressed and giggly girls in the middle of the auditorium. George muttered "Fuck this shit" again and slouched grumpily.

"When I applied for this job," Mr. Shenck began, "I told the people at the Board of Education that there were two reasons why I wanted it. The first, I said, was the fact that Bingham High School has the most sharp, professional, dedicated, bright, professional staff of any high school that I have ever had anything to do with. The teachers, the administrators, and coaches of our high school have a lot to be proud of, and each and every one of you students should be thankful for having them."

Luke stood up clapping but sat down again almost immediately when he saw that few of his classmates were in the mood to give their teachers a standing ovation. George slumped deeper in his seat.

"The second reason why I applied for this job," Mr. Shenck continued, "is you—the class of 1980. I mean that sincerely, and when I say something, you can rest assured I mean it. If you make me proud, and do what you are supposed to do, and I praise you for that, you can believe it. And by the same token, if you break the rules and let me down, and I yell at you and tell you I'm disappointed, you can believe that, too. I'm not going to mince words with you."

He shook his index finger sternly at us as he made this pledge, an I-know-how-to-deal-with-punks gesture that seemed over-dramatic, considering the general enthusiasm of the audience. I watched one boy shake his finger back discreetly, but that was the closest anyone came to heckling.

"As I was saying, the second reason I applied for this job is you, the sensational seniors of 1980. Throughout your career at Bingham, you have made a record for yourselves that others have noticed. You have the highest attendance record that this school system has seen in years. You have one of the highest academic records, with a grade average that would make a lot of other principals jealous. You have one of the best records of proper social behavior—"

Just as he said this, someone sitting behind us belched loudly, setting off a giggle chain reaction that swept through the auditorium. Mr. Shenck didn't miss a beat:

"—with the exception of a small, rude minority that doesn't know how to behave in public." He glared at the back of the auditorium. The giggles ceased.

"Before we begin to pass out the hats," Mr. Shenck continued, "I would like to make one more announcement. Because I think so highly of you, at the Athletic Assembly this Friday, and at all other assemblies held in the gymnasium, you will be allowed to sit where and with whom you want. You will no longer be required to sit in the seats assigned to your homeroom. I ask only that you remain in the bleachers on the far side of the white line, to the left as you go in, that are reserved for seniors. I am confident that you will do so, and that you will stay out of the sections assigned to the sophomores and the juniors, where you have no business being."

This announcement set off truly wild applause, which eventually turned into a standing ovation. You might have thought, to judge by the crowd's reaction, that Mr. Shenck had just canceled classes for the rest of the year. Partially unrestricted seating privileges at pep assemblies seemed like pretty small potatoes to me. But who was I to judge? I looked over at George and his friends to see what our row's official reaction to this business was going to be. They weren't applauding, and they certainly weren't standing up, so I didn't either.

When the clamor died down, the hat ceremony itself began. Senior hats, I later discovered, were an important tradition at Bingham High. For as long as anyone could remember, seniors had been given purple hats at the beginning of the year. They were allowed to wear them at school "on Fridays, at pep assemblies and during certain special activities," according to my handbook. Tradition dictated that the hats be decorated with purple and gold feathers and amusing lapel buttons. In the old days, a "Senior Hat Dance" had been held in the gymnasium at the end of the first week of school, but this custom had fallen out of favor at some point in the early seventies—at about the same time my old high school was getting rid of its prom and was nominating boys and inanimate objects for homecoming queen. At no point, however, had the hats themselves been abandoned.

The other classes had their own, lesser traditions. Juniors were allowed to purchase class rings, engraved with their year of graduation; the school handbook stipulated that the juniors wear their rings "so that the writing around the stone is facing them. When they become seniors, the ring is inverted so that the writing faces out." Lowly sophomores had to content themselves with sophomore pins, "gold ovals, around the outer borders of which is written, in raised letters, 'Bingham High School.' Attached by a chain is an additional gold pin consisting of numerals showing the year of graduation." When I was at Bingham, a fairly large number of students wore as much of this paraphernalia as they were entitled to; now that gold prices have skyrocketed, the traditions may have changed. (Class-ring manufacturers have now mostly abandoned gold in favor of inexpensive alloys with names like "shinium" and "silveroid.")

However attractive the tenth- and eleventh-grade jewelry might be, senior hats were the top of the heap. Some of the kids had been looking forward to this day for years, hoarding wacky pins and old campaign buttons so they could decorate their hats in the proper style. I could see several students clutching Baggies full of stick-on souvenirs. A couple of girls in the center section were already bartering odd lots and duplicates.

Distributing the hats ought to have been simple, since they were all the same size and looked exactly alike. But there are ways and ways of doing things. One of the assistant principals, Mr. Shenck said, had spent "a considerable number of hours over the summer" pinning the names of individual students into individual hats. Every student would thus receive a particular hat. We gave the assistant principal a hand. Representatives from the homerooms walked to the edge of the stage as their names were called and picked up the hats assigned to their groups. They flipped them over, called out the names pinned inside, and handed them out.

So many of the small activities that fill a school day are nothing more than concealed forms of attendance-taking— surveys from the nurse's office, questionnaires from the principal. When the homeroom representatives had finished handing out their hats, the administrators on the stage had a clear record of the students who were not at the assembly. The assistant principal took all unclaimed hats to a table in the corner of the stage and turned them over one by one, copying down the names still pinned inside. The twenty or thirty students who had decided the assembly period would be a good time to smoke a cigarette or a joint or run out for something to eat before going back to work had been caught.

It was unclear what this portended for me and for George and the other boys in our row; none of us had received a hat. I was left out because I hadn't been around the previous year, when the assistant principal made her list. George and the others, presumably, just didn't want their hats. It remained to be seen what, if anything, would happen to them.

"Now, seniors," said our class president, "it is time to put on your hats. We'll all do it at the same time. Before you do, take out the slip of paper inside your hat which is the 'Senior Hat Pledge.' We'll all read it together and then put on our hats."

Everyone stood, including, reluctantly, my row. The rest of our classmates recited the pledge:

"I accept this Senior Hat in knowledge of the traditions behind it, and with a promise to uphold all that it stands for. My hat represents my loyalty to Bingham High School, to its teachers and its students and its teams. I will wear it proudly on Fridays, at pep assemblies, at games, and on all other occasions when the wearing of Senior Hats is appropriate. As I wear my hat I will be ever mindful of the motto of Bingham High School, Lux Effulgeat, Let the Light Shine."

"All right, seniors . . . PUT ON YOUR HATS!"

Submarine Sandwich W/Lettuce, Tomato & Pickles, Vegetable Soup Cup, Potato Chips, Chilled Fruit Medley, Oatmeal Cookie. That's what I had on my tray. I wasn't sure whether Vegetable Soup Cup was included in the seventy-cent tab for a basic lunch, but hang the expense. I had been in line for more than ten minutes, I didn't have anybody to talk to, I was tired, and I was hungry.

Although getting my hands on a tray of food had taken some effort, simply making my way to the cafeteria had been an even greater ordeal. Not because I didn't know where the place was; by now I did. The problem was that "unsupervised transit" to and from the cafeteria is expressly forbidden at Bingham High. If you don't want to risk being nailed by a roving hall vigilante, you have to be accompanied by a teacher or a legitimate deputy of same. In my case this had meant being herded through the halls, along with the twenty other kids in my fifth-period study hall, by Mr. Derby, our teacher. When our assigned lunch period rolled around, Mr. Derby led us out into the hall, locked the door of our classroom with one of the ten thousand keys that dangled from a device that looked like a fishing reel attached to his belt, and then followed along a few paces behind us so he could nab anybody who tried to bolt the pack.

Fifth period at Bingham is a double period, an hour and a half long. If you are in Lunch Group One, you eat during the first twenty minutes, and then go to class for the rest of the period. If

you are in Lunch Group Two, you go to class for the first twenty
minutes, eat lunch for the second twenty minutes, and then go
back to class. Lunch Group Three does the same thing twenty
minutes later. The reason the kids have to eat in shifts is that
there isn't enough room in the cafeteria for all of them to be
there at the same time. My study hall was in Lunch Group Two,
so we had twenty minutes to kill before the schedule said we
could eat. These twenty minutes we spent listening to Mr. Derby
tell us how he intended to run his study hall.

"For the time being," he said, "this will be an open study hall,
which means that you can talk *quietly* with your neighbor. But
if the talking gets out of hand, I reserve the right to lay down the
law, and if that happens anybody who so much as sneezes
without my written permission is going to wish he'd never been
born." On that note, we had gone to lunch.

I have not often felt more alone and out of place than I did
after I had paid for my food and walked out into the cafeteria
proper to find a place to eat. As I looked out over table after table
of new schoolmates I did not see a single face I remembered even
vaguely from earlier in the day. The other kids in my fifth-
period study hall had disappeared entirely. George Menaro was
either not present or in hiding. I didn't even see any teachers I
recognized; they were all off in the faculty dining room, eating
in peace. I walked slowly down the center aisle, eyes scanning
first to the right, then to the left. I had no idea what I would do if
I couldn't find a likely place to put down my tray; there didn't
seem to be an empty table anywhere, so eating by myself wasn't
even a possibility. I passed a block of all-black tables, and a
section where virtually everyone was wearing a senior hat.
Oddly enough, there didn't seem to be any coed tables. The boys
and the girls were keeping to themselves. A full third of the
girls weren't even eating. They sat glumly at trayless tables,
staring straight ahead and not talking: dieters.

Just as I got to the end of the aisle, I spotted two boys who had been in my study hall and went over and sat with them. Neither looked up. I opened my carton of chocolate milk on the wrong side and had to pick little pieces of soggy paper out of my mouth after I took a sip.

The two boys, both of whom were wearing leather jackets, were talking about the principal. Mr. Shenck's appointment had apparently caused some concern among Bingham's tough guys. When Mr. Shenck himself walked by a little later, I pointed to him and asked my lunchmates if that was the principal. I figured the question would identify me as a newcomer and possibly open up a little conversation.

"Yeah, that's him," one of the boys said, adding, "the fucker."

This was the last word either of them uttered, to me or to each other. A few minutes later they loaded up their trays and carried them over to the dishwasher's window in the wall near the food line.

It did not immediately occur to me that there might be a reason for their haste. I had not yet figured out how the lunch shifts worked, and although I knew I was supposed to meet up with Mr. Derby eventually, I did now know when. In fact, I did not know where. Before entering the cafeteria we had gathered briefly by the bank of lavatories, and I assumed that when we finally met up again it would be there. But I wasn't sure how to get back.

I had to do something soon, however. More and more students were taking back their trays and disappearing into the halls. I looked with mixed emotions at my largely uneaten submarine sandwich and then carried it and the rest of my lunch over to the tray dump.

As I turned the corner just outside the cafeteria, I caught a glimpse of Mr. Derby at the foot of the stairs at the far end of the hall. I tagged along at a distance and slipped into the crowd when he unlocked the door of our classroom.

So much for lunch. I wished I had thought to stick my oatmeal cookie in my pocket before turning in my tray, but it was too late to do anything about that. And besides, school would be over in another two hours.

Meanwhile, I had other things to worry about. Friends, for example, and when I was going to start making a few. I hadn't had much luck so far at winning my way into my classmates' hearts. George Menaro was all right as far as he went, but he definitely had limitations, not the least of which was the fact that he didn't like me.

Just as I was thinking this, I felt someone tap me on the shoulder. When I turned around, the girl sitting in the desk behind mine ducked down so that the girl sitting behind her could see over her back.

She smiled and whispered, "What's your name?"

She didn't want to know any more than that, my name, but her question carried me through the rest of the day. When school ended I took a long walk around the neighborhood. I found the town library (in the façade of which are four stained-glass windows, dedicated to Plato, Emerson, Victor Hugo, and Dante), the nearest Burger King, a bowling alley, a movie theater, a shopping center. After an hour or so of aimless wandering I passed a neighborhood bar on a secondary road about a mile from school. Ah, I thought, just what I need. The day had warmed up considerably, and a beer or two would taste good. I could sit at a little table, and make a few notes, and think about my day.

I was almost through the door before I remembered: The only identification I had was a phony birth certificate that said I was seventeen years old. What if they proofed me? And what if one of my teachers saw me? I went into a little convenience store about halfway down the block and bought a Coke and a bag of potato chips.

3
∾Cheetos

When I got home again after that first day, I was both excited and disappointed—excited because I had survived an entire day without being caught, and disappointed because my classmates hadn't knocked themselves over trying to get to know me.

"How did it go?" my wife asked.

"Fine," I said.

"Did you make any friends?"

I debated whether to lie. "Oh, nothing much," I said finally. "Just a girl who practically raped me in study hall."

"Well," Ann said, "if you want to do something about that, go right ahead; I give you my complete permission."

"That wasn't what I meant," I said. "Actually, I didn't make many friends at all. Or any, for that matter."

"It's still very early."

"I sort of made one friend, but he doesn't like me."

"That's a nice start, anyway. You can be *his* friend."

"I had lunch with two hoods."

"There you go."

"They weren't big conversationalists. And no one remembered to give me a Senior Hat."

A friend of ours who had just moved to New York came over for dinner, and the three of us spent the evening cutting up brown paper bags to make covers for my school books.

Because I took the train to and from Bingham almost every day, I sometimes worried that one of my classmates would spot me at the station and begin to wonder where I spent the night. Fortunately, my morning train arrived half an hour before school began, and my afternoon train left more than two hours after it let out. This gave me a fairly wide margin of safety. On the few occasions when I did run into students I knew, I was able to talk my way out of what might have been uncomfortable situations.

One evening in the first weeks of school I found eight of my classmates, six boys and two girls, sitting on the station platform when I arrived to catch my train back to New York. They were dangling their legs over the track and sharing a bottle of wine. I considered slipping out the back and waiting for a later train, but before I could make a move toward the parking lot, one of the boys noticed me and beckoned me over with the bottle. His name, which I couldn't think of at the time, was Greg Liszk. He was tall and heavyset and had extremely blond hair. We were in the same math class, and I had accidentally won his gratitude the week before by not covering up my paper when he leaned over to look at it during a quiz. I sat down next to him and took a sip of wine.

Greg and his friends were going to a Who concert in New York. They had bought their tickets by mail many weeks before. Greg assumed that I was going to the concert, too. When he asked where my seat was, I mumbled something about having to visit an aunt in Brooklyn. It wasn't a very good lie, but no one paid any attention. The concert was too much on everyone's mind.

One of Greg's friends said that a friend of his in another town had camped out with his girl friend for seven straight nights in the parking lot of a record store where tickets were going to go on sale. They didn't get quite the seats they were hoping for, though, because there were something like a hundred people ahead of them in the line.

The Who concert was a big deal. There was a rumor at Bingham that the tour it was a part of might be the Who's last. Because the performance was on a school night, Greg had practically had to beg his parents for permission to go. He had also had to make excuses to the manager of the A&P where he worked four nights a week. Most of the other kids had had to make similar arrangements. But seeing the Who was worth all the trouble. After all, there might never be a chance to see them in concert again.

I had been to a Who concert in Kansas City ten years before, and even then it had been a big deal. The tickets cost more than the tickets for any concert I had ever been to: five dollars. The concert hall where the band appeared was an old roller-skating rink that had been bought by a group of long-haired entrepreneurs and turned into a would-be Fillmore Midwest called Freedom Palace. There were no seats. The poured-concrete floor was covered with an acre of flame-retardant plastic grass, and everybody sat or stood or danced on that. Freedom Palace was almost always crowded, but on the night of the Who concert it was especially so: Someone had printed up and sold several hundred counterfeit tickets. Fire marshals waded in and out of the crowd and threatened to close down the show if people didn't move out of the fire lanes. Sometime the day before, the air-conditioning system had broken down, and now one of the long-haired entrepreneurs climbed onto the stage to announce that it was 103 degrees inside the building and getting hotter. He said there were registered nurses on duty in the back of the hall and anyone overcome by heat would be taken care of.

The memory of Woodstock was achingly fresh at that time, and when the announcer mentioned the registered nurses, you could almost see lightbulbs clicking on in the minds of the people in the crowd. Registered nurses! A hundred and three degrees! Things, clearly, were going to be as grim as they had been at the Festival of Peace and Love. Quite possibly someone would die, or a baby would be born. A wave of euphoria swept across the crowd. If someone had gone to the microphone at that point and told everyone to steer clear of the brown acid, the entire audience would have been lifted bodily into heaven. People in different parts of the hall began peeling out of their clothes. Two of the long-haired entrepreneurs, running the light show from a console high above the floor, emptied buckets of ice onto the crowd. Every few seconds a chunk of ice would smack somebody hard on top of the head, and you would hear a cry of pain. When the backup band (Johnny Winter, I think) started playing, a girl across the auditorium stood up, took off her shirt, dramatically wrung the perspiration from it, and began to dance. She waved the shirt with both hands over her head, bare breasts slapping against her ribs a half beat in back of the music.

It was an awesome moment. I felt almost unbearably elated. My friends and I were a part of something big and important and fully incomprehensible to our parents. That was what made it so powerful. It was possible to believe that merely by sweating out this particular Who concert you were not only advancing the cause of rock and roll but also ending the war in Vietnam, driving a stake into the heart of Richard Nixon, and putting a few dents in the old man's brand-new car. A few of the people in the crowd became nearly irate when the Who declined to play along with the fantasy and threatened to leave the stage if something wasn't done about the heat.

The train was fifteen minutes late. A conductor explained that there was trouble on the line and that we would be experiencing further delays all the way to New York. One of Greg's friends was worried that there might not be time to eat dinner before the concert. "Who needs food?" Greg said. They had all been drinking steadily since school let out. Greg had what he claimed was a case of beer concealed about his person, and every ten minutes or so he would pull a fresh can out of his fatigue jacket and pop the top. Both the girls had leather-and-plastic wineskins strung over their shoulders. Several of the boys were carrying pints of whiskey. Greg handed me a beer and said, "Drink up." A boy named Ed had already drunk most of a pint of Southern Comfort. He had also drained a lot of the bottle of wine and smoked one of Greg's joints without sharing it. I watched him tip back his head and polish off the last few ounces in his bottle. He didn't even shudder. His cheeks were drained of color, and his eyes were glazed and drooping. *He* didn't know it yet, but I could see from the way his lower lip was hanging that he had drunk so much he would eventually be very sick. I found myself in a position that must be familiar to parents: I could foresee dire consequences but was powerless to intervene. Fifteen minutes into the trip, Ed hoisted himself from his seat and addressed the other passengers.

"Hear the word of the Lord," he slurred. "Hear the word of the Lord. You are about to hear the most profound thing you will ever hear. This is true, true, true. Everybody please be quiet. You are going to hear the profound word of the Lord. I am the Lord and I am speaking to you."

"Sit down, Ed," Greg said.

"Do not interrupt the Lord. Hear the word of the Lord. The Lord is about to make his profound announcement."

"Ed, you're drunk."

"Fuckfuckfuckfuckfuckfuckfuckfuckfuckfuckfuckfuckfuckfuck."

"Sit down, Ed!"

"You have now heard the word of the Lord. The Lord thanks you for your attention."

I looked around to see if any of the passengers were upset, but no one seemed to mind. Even drunk, Ed didn't look very frightening. He was about five feet nine and had curly brown hair and an elfin face with a youthfully formless nose. He was wearing a faded denim jacket and a black T-shirt that had THE WHO on the front underneath a blurry silk-screened picture of the band. Black T-shirts with the names of rock bands printed on them have joined blue jeans and sneakers as obligatory articles in the wardrobes of teenagers. Everyone in our group on the train (except for me, alas) was wearing one. Some of the boys in my class wore them virtually every day to school. Many would have felt naked at a rock concert without one. The shirts are like military decorations commemorating famous campaigns: They are physical evidence that you have been someplace worth being. They also make a plain statement about your musical loyalties: To wear a shirt emblazoned with the picture of a bad or generally disregarded band (Kiss, for instance, if you are older than thirteen or fourteen) is to commit social suicide.

Ed staggered toward the front of the train. "I'm going to the smoking car," he shouted. Greg pulled another beer out of his jacket and handed it to me. "Ed just decided today that he was going to get totally fucked up," he said, "and so that's what he did." Greg didn't seem too much the worse for wear, even though he had drunk four or five beers since boarding the train. "We've got to finish this crap before we get to New York," he said, "because they won't let you inside the auditorium with booze."

Ed came sailing back down the aisle and bounced off in the opposite direction. He paused at the door and said, "Hello, everyone. Hello, ma'am. I am totally fucked up. I would offer you to get fucked up, too, but I have drank up all my liquor." He then pulled the door back just far enough to let himself through and stepped into the open space between the cars. I could see him through the window in the door. He was having trouble keeping his balance. Every time the train lurched, his body responded with comic exaggeration. "Watch him get himself killed," someone said. Finally he threw his weight against the far door and disappeared into the other car. The girl he had been sitting next to returned with his jacket draped over her arm. "Give me that," Greg said. He tossed it up onto the luggage rack. On the back of his jacket Ed had written "Ted Nugent #1" in white paint. "Now nobody tell him where it is," Greg said, and he opened another beer.

There were several jackets like Ed's at Bingham High School. One of the girls had spelled out "Grateful Dead" with brass studs on the back of a denim vest. A boy had bought some felt letters at Woolworth's and had his mother sew the words "Rock and Roll" on the back of his jacket. The names of individual rock bands and performers have a great power that sometimes rubs off on the people who utter them or copy them out on a piece of paper. One day in accounting, I watched a bored boy carefully writing the names of his favorite bands in fancy handwriting on a sheet of notebook paper. "Charlie Daniels Band," he wrote. "Led Zeppelin." He made the letters by moving his blue ball-point pen back and forth in tight zigzags, so that the result looked slightly out of focus. You could tell by his expression that he was thinking his kind of writing might not look too bad on an album cover. There were boys in my class who filled page after page in their notebooks with the signatures of rock stars, sometimes slanting the letters to the right, sometimes leaning them back to the left, one time making an A so that it looked like a little star. One boy I knew had a spiral notebook on the cover of which he had written, each in a different hand, the names of his favorite bands. In the middle of the arrangement, surrounded by a jagged halo, was the word "MATH."

A rock star is an idol tailor-made for a teenager. No other

cultural hero is quite so accessible while at the same time exercising such enormous power. A rock star can be as ugly as Frank Zappa or as scrawny as Jimmy Page. He's cool in spite of himself. Others have pointed out that the rock kingdom contains a disproportionately large number of people who bombed socially in high school. Rock and roll is the last best hope of teenage nurds. Janis Joplin's triumphant, pathetic return to the Texas high school where she had been an outcast as a student was, for her, the ultimate act of revenge. Thousands of adolescents dream of doing the same thing. For boys what is important is not that rock stars are sex symbols but that they are sexual avengers; they keep playing while the girls roll in the aisles. They get even. An electric guitar is an awesome instrument, a weapon for lashing back at the people who make life difficult for you. And its hold over a boy dies very slowly; I once caught a college professor of mine raptly picking out a solo on an imaginary guitar in accompaniment to a Rolling Stones record.

Ed appeared once again through the door of the car. He was carrying half a dozen bags of Cheetos, one of which he tossed to Greg and me. "There's a bar car up at the front of the train," he said. "I tried to buy some beer but asshole wouldn't sell me any because I ain't old enough and I was already drunk." He turned to the other passengers. "Now, tell me, do I look drunk? Do I look pissfuckingincapacitatedlyshitfaced? Tell me honestly."

"You look perfectly sober," a businessman said.

"Thank you, sir. Thank you very much. Here. Have a bag of Cheetos." He aimed wide, missing the man by several seats. The bag landed in the lap of a young woman. "I am sorry, madam," Ed said. "I am sorry to have inconvenienced you with a bag of cheese snacks." He collapsed into his seat and put his arm around the girl beside him.

"Marry me, my sweet," he sighed.

Some aspects of American youth culture have proved surprisingly durable over the last ten years. The most popular rock bands at Bingham when I was there were, by and large, ones my friends and I had followed a decade before: the Grateful Dead, the Rolling Stones, the Who, Led Zeppelin, Fleetwood Mac, the Allman Brothers, Jethro Tull, several others. Occasionally people mentioned newer names—Foreigner, the Cars, the Clash—but the real stars were the old favorites. Before enrolling at Bingham I had wondered whether I would have to give myself a crash course in new teenage music, but only rarely did I hear anyone talking about a band I wasn't familiar with. Even the songs hadn't changed. At a Jethro Tull concert in October, the encore number was a song recorded when I was in ninth grade.

What has changed, of course, is the cultural and political significance of the various bands and their music. Rock music was once an important symbolic element of a general political attitude. Attendance at a rock concert was a minor act of political rebellion, a statement of allegiance to a radical idea. The same is not true today, even though a lot of the old performers are still going strong. Part of the reason is money. A mainstream rock band today occupies roughly the same position in the culture as a professional football team. Led Zeppelin and the Pittsburgh Steelers drift together in a vague continuum of big money, fast cars, and prestige. Rock concerts are a major spectator sport. They provide an opportunity to get very drunk and very high, make a lot of noise, and tap into tbe sexual current that throbs through popular music. Any rebellion is of the purely adolescent kind, the sort that prickles at strict parietals and recessionary allowances. The black T-shirts the kids wear are like overblown baseball cards. Unlike blue jeans, whose symbolic importance derives at base from their incomparable practicality, black T-shirts are pure status, pure consumption.

The class of 1980's weakness for the music of the sixties was by no means all-inclusive. No one, for instance, ever mentioned Motown. Soul music has lately experienced something of a resurgence, but it hadn't hit Bingham when I was there. In fact, the white students at Bingham almost without exception listened only to music made by white performers. When I was in junior high school, the music on the stereo at almost every party I went to was predominately soul: the Supremes, the Temptations, Aretha Franklin, the Four Tops, Gladys Knight, Junior Walker. At Bingham, the musical tastes of the black and white students nowhere overlapped. The music of the black students was disco. And among white students, the near-unanimous opinion was that "disco sucks."

I looked across the aisle at Ed. His face was frozen in an expression of horrified self-absorption. His skin was absolutely without color. He rose slowly and stumbled toward the front of the train in silence.

"Hey, where's he going?" Greg asked.

There was no answer. The girl Ed had been sitting next to moved across the aisle to an empty seat beside another friend.

Thirty minutes later, as we were approaching the station, Ed had not returned. Greg and some of the others debated jokingly about whether to leave him on the train and let him fend for himself. Finally Greg got up to go look for him. He returned a few minutes later. Ed was behind him, falling against the seats on either side. He was smiling gamely. His lower lip glistened.

"He ralphed," Greg said.

Everyone laughed.

"Did you really ralph?"

"He ralphed!"

"Look! It's all over his leg!" There was a wide orange swath down the side of his pants.

"It's the Cheetos!"
"Who's gotta sit next to him at the concert?"
"Not me!"
"He really ralphed!"
"Oh, Christ! *I'm* sitting next to him!"
"Me, too!"
"It's gonna be a fucking long night!"
"I can't believe he really ralphed!"
"Brother, did he!"
"Oh, Christ!"
"It's the Cheetos!"

4
⁓ P.E.

Clothes, in the peculiar idiom of physical education teachers, are known as "street clothes." Any shoe not specifically designed to promote traction, speed, or maneuverability, is called a "street shoe." The labels bespeak a quaint ignorance, as though physical education teachers were at a loss to describe precisely what it is that people do when they are not engaged in physical education.

It was the second Tuesday of the school year, and although we were not yet engaged in physical education, we were about to be. I was sitting in the bleachers of the Bingham gymnasium along with sixty or seventy of my schoolmates, half of them boys and half of them girls. The girls, for the most part, were keeping to themselves. All but a few were sitting in the next bank of bleachers, on the other side of the scoreboard. Even from a distance it was possible to see that all was not well with them. They were fidgeting in their seats. They were talking to one another in hushed and nervous tones. It was the first day of gym. We had just been given our "street locker" assignments, had just returned from testing the padlocks we had been issued. The girls in the next bank of bleachers were clutching the tiny slips of paper on which their combinations had been written as though they were Mafia hit contracts filled out in their own names.

Girls do not like gym. They don't like anything about it. They don't like taking their clothes off in front of other girls, they don't like squeezing their bodies into embarrassing little uniforms, they don't like feeling their armpits fill with sweat. Gym would be bad enough if it were all girls—bad enough because girl jocks are possibly even less forgiving of physical incompetence than boy jocks—but *coed* gym is such a gruesome idea that the female mind aborts it instantly, and coed gym is now the law of the land. A sinister piece of legislation called Title IX makes it illegal to give either sex special treatment in P.E., and the girls do not like it. If a high school were a sort of Girls' Inferno, coed gym would be the ninth circle, the sprawling lake of frozen shit on the absolute floor of hell.

The girls were feeling doubly damned at the moment because everyone in the class had just been handed a three-by-five index card and asked to fill it out with name, homeroom number, and top three choices, in order of preference, for a section assignment for the fall semester. There were four sections, comprising four different combinations of activities: Group One—Soccer, Speedball, Volleyball, Universal Gym; Group Two—Field Hockey, Racquetball, Basketball, Conditioning; Group Three—Floor Hockey, Paddle Tennis, Open Gym, Conditioning; Group Four —Golf, Table Tennis, Floor Activity, Open Gym. All right now, girls, what'll it be, the boiling oil, the guillotine, the gas chamber, or the electric chair.

Well, not quite. There was a way out, and virtually all of the girls were going to try to take it. They were going to write "Group Four" on their cards, with no second or third choice, because the activities in Group Four were the only ones in which students were allowed to participate while wearing "street clothes." The only suiting up they would have to do would be to put on a pair of sneakers.

But there was a problem. Group Four had only enough room for maybe two-thirds of the girls in the class, and that was assuming that none of the boys felt inclined to spend their gym periods toning up their chip shots, or putting an edge on their Ping-Pong serves. Even considering the fact that a small handful of girls would probably sign up for field hockey or soccer *of their own free will,* there still wasn't going to be enough room in Group Four for all the girls who wanted desperately to be in it.

"If I don't get in," one girl said, "I'm gonna go complain to Mr. Shenck."

"We should all go," another girl said.

When all the cards had been filled out and handed back, the four gym teachers, two men and two women, sorted them into piles and conferred quietly for a moment behind the portable blackboard on which the four sections had been listed and described. The girls' half of the bleachers was buzzing like a hive. A girl in the front row was wringing her hands.

The gym teachers stepped forward. A young woman in a yellow warm-up suit was the first to speak.

"In assigning you to groups," she said, "we tried to do so according to preference. In cases where this was impossible" —wholesale gasping and moaning—"priority was given to upperclassmen. The following students have been assigned to Group Four and will report to me."

As she read off the names on the cards in her hand, the girls were deathly still. When a girl heard her name called she would uncross her fingers, or sink into her seat, or look up at the ceiling and offer a brief and silent prayer of thanks. But as the list of names grew longer, the girls who had not been called began to squirm. When the teacher in the yellow warm-ups read the final name, there was a brief hush and then a loud, agonized scream: "OHHHHHHH MYYYYYYYYY GODDDDDDDDD!!!!!!"

I was placed in Group One, my first choice. When my name was called I crossed the basketball floor to where the other kids in the section were being divided into six-person squads. The squads were not teams, our teacher said; we wouldn't choose those until we began to play. The squad assignments were intended merely to make attendance-taking easier.

Our teacher was Mr. Meiden, who was also the football coach. He was tall and strong and about fifty years old. His hair was short and gray. He was wearing a light blue short-sleeved polyester sport shirt, a wide white belt, dark blue pants, and black ripple-soled shoes—another vestigial uniform. On the chair beside him was a purple windbreaker with the words "Bingham High School Coaching Staff" over the left breast.

"Remember that six unexcused absences will give you an F," he told us. He looked at the five or six girls in the section. "If you are here but not dressed and don't have a note from your doctor, that counts as an unexcused absence."

The other kids in my squad were Frank Beauchamp, Jennifer Hughes, Gary Meyer, John Finley, and Les Zulinski. Les, I already knew, was the quarterback of the football team. He was also in my psychology class, and he and I had joked around amiably on several occasions before or after class. He was big and handsome and a genuine teenage heartthrob—the girls wouldn't leave him alone. He didn't have to take P.E., since he was on a team and therefore had practice every day, but he went anyway, because, he said, he liked the opportunity to "loosen up" in the middle of the day.

The other kids in the squad were strangers. Most of them were juniors, I later found out. Jennifer, the only girl, was quite heavy and not at all athletic-looking. She had short red hair of the sort that can never quite be cajoled into style: not straight, not wavy, not anything. I figured that she had already decided she could live with an F in gym and that none of us would ever see her again. But it turned out that Group One had been her first choice.

Mr. Meiden sent us back over to the bleachers to wait out the rest of the period. Because we were all still dressed for "the street," he couldn't in good conscience let us fill the time by shooting baskets. Les and I sat together in the first row and talked about Mr. Chapin, our psychology teacher.

"One day," Les said, "all the guys on the baseball team got together before practice and decided to strike out every time they came to bat. They all just kept stepping up to the plate and swinging and never getting a hit. Chapin went out of his fucking mind. One of the guys told him that the bats were all crooked, and that's why they couldn't hit anything. So Chapin picked up one of the damn things and held it up to the light to see if it really was. It was *hysterical*."

Sitting on the other side of Les was a short, skinny black kid with thick glasses and immense brown oxford shoes. One of the other black kids in the class, a big muscular guy with one silver earring, kept walking back and forth in front of him and stepping on his shoes. He tried to pull his feet up close to the front of the bleachers, but the big guy kept landing on his toes.

"Hey, cut that out," Les said.

The big guy took a long hard look at Les, made one last swipe at the oxfords, and strutted away.

"What a fuckhead," Les said.

The little guy took a big black notebook out of his briefcase and opened it across his lap. It was filled with drawings.

"Did you do those?" Les asked.

He nodded.

Les took the notebook and flipped through the pages. "These are really good," he said. The drawings were all in comic-book style, drawn with a black ball-point pen. In one panel an immense superhero was holding a dozen villains at bay with a raygun. The hero was drawn the way all boys draw comic-book heroes: with muscles unknown to science and arms a foot too short. The hero's left hand was hanging at about waist level, instead of midthigh, where it belonged. Les turned to the first page. Written painstakingly across the top of it in large shaded letters was: "Strange Comix Presents MASTERMAN." A little farther down it said: "Every man longs to escape from the world of INSANITY into the world of INFINITY." Below this was "Created, Written, and Drawn by Michael Raymond Jensen."

"These are good, Mike," Les said. "Did you think it all up yourself?"

Mike nodded and smiled. "I never had lessons," he half whispered.

In the first panel of the series, MASTERMAN (who had a capital M on his forehead) was conferring with an ordinary mortal. "Greetings, Sire," the mortal was saying. "I bring much needed news of the infidels."

"I can see by your face," said MASTERMAN, "that this news is not good. Follow me into my private chamber. You will not find it wanting." MASTERMAN, I noticed, was white.

Soon after that the period ended. Before it did, Mr. Carlut, the head of the physical education program, made an announcement to the entire class:

"I will remind you, ladies and gentlemen, that you must have a uniform on Thursday. Is there anyone here who does not have a uniform? We have some old trunks in the lost and found, if any of the boys need them. And there's a box of old stuff for the girls. There will be no excuse for not having a uniform on Thursday. If there's a financial problem—if you can't afford a uniform just now—let us know and we'll buy you one." He paused. "Am I to understand by your silence that you all have your uniforms? And that you will be wearing them on Thursday? Is that the case? Then unless you come to see me after class about having a little help to buy one, I will assume that each and every one of you, with the exception of the Group Fours, will be suited up and ready to go. Understood?"

The girls could only groan.

Wednesday night, at home in New York, I dropped my fork in the middle of dinner.

"What's the matter?" Ann asked.

"I don't have a *uniform*," I said.

Leaving her in utter puzzlement, I ran out of our apartment, took a cab downtown, and bought a pair of five-dollar gym shorts just as the store was closing.

The next day Mr. Meiden divided us into teams. About half the kids in our section either had not shown up or had forgotten to bring their gym shorts, so the teams were small. Les, Frank Beauchamp, Jennifer Hughes, and I were on one team, along with a couple of kids from the other squads. One of them was a pudgy black girl who was wearing a long raincoat over her shorts and T-shirt.

"I don't think you'll need the raincoat," Mr. Meiden said. "The last I heard it wasn't raining."

Everybody laughed. The black girl said nothing, but she kept the coat on.

There were four fairly sinister-looking hoods in our section. None of them had suited up. They were lounging around in the bleachers on the other side of the gym, not paying attention to what was going on. Mr. Meiden called them over to where the rest of us were. They got up slowly and stretched a little, then ambled across the gym, scuffing the heels of their motorcycle boots on the floor. They were all wearing black leather jackets.

"If you guys want F's in here," Mr. Meiden said, "that's okay with me. But whether you suit up or not you've got to stay with us when we form our squads and you've got to go outside when we go out to play. And I can tell you one thing: Even with a big bad leather coat on, it's gonna be a heck of a lot warmer out there if you're getting a little exercise."

When we went outside, the hoods hung back. Mr. Meiden told us all to stop at the street, because there was a school rule against letting students walk through traffic unsupervised. We were all waiting at the crosswalk when he came jogging out of the building.

"Hurry up," Les called. "We're being run over."

"I don't doubt it for a minute, Les."

Mr. Meiden led us over onto the practice field. The hoods turned off to the right and walked slowly around the cinder track. When they got to the far turn, they stopped and huddled together for a minute. Little plumes of smoke billowed up over their heads. Mr. Meiden saw what was going on—he stood and looked for a long time with his hands on his hips, shaking his head—but decided not to do anything about it. As we were standing there, the Group Four kids filed past us on their way to an impromptu driving range on the other side of the field. The teacher in the yellow warm-ups was carrying a beat-up canvas golf bag filled with five irons and a bucket of practice balls. About twenty girls shuffled along dejectedly behind her. At the back of the pack was Mike Jensen, the comic-book artist, the only boy in the group.

No one in my group, of course, wanted to be goalie. After a lot of general hemming and hawing, Les volunteered on our side and Mr. Meiden conscripted a junior on the other. I told Les I'd spell him when he got bored.

"I was going to give you a big lecture on technique," Mr. Meiden said, "but why don't you just play along for a while and I'll give you pointers as we go."

Our team got off to a quick lead. Frank Beauchamp, it turned out, was something of a soccer star, as was another kid on our team, a big boy named Tom, who had long brown hair. They marched the ball down the field together again and again and sailed it past the goalie a couple of times. The goals were marked with orange rubber highway pylons placed about ten feet apart. Every time the ball came down to our end of the field, the goalie on the other team nudged his pylons a foot or two closer together. The girl in the raincoat and I hung back to play defense. We weren't a very effective screen, but Les stopped every ball that came to him.

When the score was 3–0, Mr. Meiden stepped in on the other team to even up the odds. Frank stole the ball away from him right in front of the goal and fired it in to make the score 4–0.

"Why don't you play on *their* team?" one of the girls asked Mr. Meiden. He chuckled and retired to the sidelines. During the rest of the game he kept up a cheerful patter of praise, directed mostly at those of us who weren't doing very well.

I relieved Les after a while but had less luck stopping balls. By the end of the game our lead had been trimmed to a single point. No one minded, though. It was a beautiful day, cool but absolutely clear, and most of the kids in soccer were glad to be outside. As time went by, P.E. actually became one of the high points of my week. If you live in New York and neither jog nor play squash, eventually you begin to feel a little guilty. Now when people asked me what I did for exercise, I'd be able to say, "Well, as a matter of fact, I'm in *gym*."

There was a big bank of showers in the boys' locker room, but we weren't allowed to use them. Somewhere along the line showers had ceased to be a part of the P.E. regimen. After our soccer game there was no way to cool off except to soak a handful of paper towels in the sink and sponge down with those. We all sat around on the benches, flapping our arms, trying to air out. I had forgotten to bring any deodorant, so I spent the rest of the day in an unsavory state.

At 12:15, when gym was over, our class went directly to lunch. As always, we had to be escorted, even though the cafeteria was just a few yards down the hall. When there were only a couple of minutes to go, people started to cluster at the door of the gym, hoping to beat the lines at the food counter. Just before the bell rang, the ten or so black kids in the class quietly muscled their way en masse through the crowd at the door so they could be first. The white kids looked the other way and stepped aside to let them pass. Most of the black guys were big and intimidating, and the consensus seemed to be that it was smarter just to let them do what they wanted.

Mike Jensen, however, hadn't noticed what was going on until well after all the other black guys had worked their way to the front. When he saw where they were he trotted across the basketball floor with his briefcase and tried to push his way in, too. Suddenly there was a lot of shoving and shouting.

"Hey, man," somebody said. *"No cuts."*

"Yeah, man, get your ass back there."

Mike put his head down and pushed, but two of the white kids took him by the shoulders and moved him to the back of the crowd. He stood there with his head down, not certain what to do. Les walked over and asked him if he was still doing his drawings, and Mike brightened a little at that, but he had still suffered a humiliating blow. The white kids hadn't been afraid of him, and the black kids hadn't stood up for him.

The incident was typical of race relations at Bingham. You could tell that the black kids and the white kids weren't quite certain what to do about each other. There were virtually no openly racial confrontations—no cries of Nigger! or Honky!—but there was a good deal of tension under the surface. The white kids were suspicious of the black kids, but by now they were sympathetic enough to the idea of racial equality to avoid the overt racism they probably saw in their parents. The black kids felt like outsiders, but, at the moment at least, there were no burning issues of the sort that provoke angry confrontations. Frustrations on both sides were vented on easy prey like Mike Jensen. He was an embarrassment to the blacks and a safe target for the whites. Guys like Les Zulinski were rare. But even Les's compassion was probably as much the result of his seamless self-confidence as of anything else.

At lunch, though, Mike won back some self-esteem. When Les and I got our trays, I saw Mike sitting at one of the black tables in the cafeteria. He had his briefcase open in front of him, and some of the other black kids were looking over his drawings. As we walked past I saw one of them pat Mike on the back.

5
∾Getting High

About the time the school year began, Angie Dickinson, on *Policewoman,* went undercover in a high school to sniff out a dangerous drug ring. I didn't watch the show, but I was afraid my new classmates might. From the very beginning I was worried that if any of the kids at Bingham got suspicious about who I was, their first guess would not be that I was a writer, but that I was a narc. I could picture myself asking some innocent question about marijuana and using a slang word that had been popular in my day but was no longer current. "Hey, man," someone would say, "no one but a cop would call weed *grass.*" Then a gang of teenage drug dealers would drag me into a corner and kick my teeth in, or something. So I decided it would be wise not to be too inquisitive. As a consequence, almost everything I learned about drug use at Bingham came to me more or less by accident, without any prompting on my part.

Actually, there wasn't an awful lot of drug use going on at Bingham when I was there. As the semester wore on, Bingham, like other parts of the country, was suffering a marijuana shortage of fairly major proportions. Good pot was going for as much as a hundred dollars an ounce, when it was available at all. Kids at schools in wealthier communities might not have batted an eye at prices like that, but a hundred dollars was a major sum for the kids at Bingham, most of whom had to work after school in order to make ends meet. Most of those who continued to buy pot had to settle for distinctly inferior stuff, which always seemed to be available for fifteen or twenty dollars an ounce. Kids who didn't feel like paying even that had yet another option, which was to pick it themselves.

"Last night me and this Puerto Rican kid went over to this place he knew about," a boy in my homeroom said one morning. "There was dope growing over there that was six feet high. It was amazing. First we had to sort of crawl past this old guy's house, but then the bastard saw us, so we booked *immediately*. We went over to this other place where the plants were just as high. We just walked around yanking them up. We must've scored twenty or thirty pounds of that stuff."

"Homegrown weed isn't worth a shit," another boy said.

"Yeah, but the price is right."

Sometimes a group of kids would band together to buy small amounts of expensive but superior marijuana that none of them could afford alone. In the cafeteria one day three hoods dropped by the table I was sitting at to ask another boy if he wanted in on a deal.

"Man," said one of the hoods, "there's this guy who's got some really incredible Hawaiian weed that he's selling for two hundred and fifty bucks an ounce. That's a lot of dough, but I swear, one toke will get you wasted."

"I don't know, man," the boy at our table said.

"It's wicked shit, man," another hood said. "All these little tops—they look like Christmas trees."

Even if there hadn't been a pot shortage, I'm not sure I would have seen or heard much about drug use. In all my time at Bingham I saw only two actual drug deals taking place, and neither was anything special, just an average kid trying to track down a little marijuana for the weekend. Once or twice I caught a whiff of marijuana in a hall or in a bathroom, but that was rare. I talked to some kids at another high school who guessed that fifty percent of their schoolmates bought marijuana on a regular basis. I think their figure is probably high (teenagers are notorious overestimators of drug use among their peers), but it's not *wildly* exaggerated. I would guess that most of my classmates at Bingham smoked marijuana at least "every once in a while," as the polls always say, and that something like a quarter or a third of them bought their own marijuana more than once every couple of years.

Use of drugs other than marijuana was far from widespread. Before history one day, a girl read aloud from a drug-abuse pamphlet she had found on the floor. One section of the pamphlet listed half a dozen supposedly common drugs—drugs that were certainly common when I was a teenager—including mescaline, psilocybin, Quaaludes, and Methedrine. Most of the kids who were listening laughed out loud, not because they thought the pamphlet was stupid but because they had never heard of the drugs. The girl who was reading couldn't even pronounce most of the names.

"Is that the one *you* take?" another girl asked.

"No," she said. "All I ever take is Bufferin."

The kids in history weren't necessarily typical, of course. But I don't think any but the very straightest kids in my old high school class would have been unfamiliar with those names. The real boom days on the exotic drug market are over. Most of what is called LSD nowadays isn't even LSD.

All of this is not to say that no one took drugs at Bingham. But most of the heavy drug use was confined to the tough-guy population, the hoods. One day I heard four of them talking about an old friend of theirs:

"Has anybody talked to Eddie?"

"I was gonna write him, man, but then I spaced it out. I was gonna tell him about Weasel."

"Everybody knows about Weasel."

"His heart stopped for like four minutes, man. It was almost the same as this other guy that drowned in his own saliva."

"There was this huge thing in the paper just about Weasel, about how he'd never be the same."

"Did you see that angel dust special on TV the other night? Made by this guy that used to be a teacher?"

"There's more than one, man. They had like two of them on in the same fucking week."

"This special was totally outrageous. They had like this jaguar that they hit up with angel dust and it fucking went out of its mind."

"There was that lady that fried her baby in oil."

"Fucking intense."

"They had this one guy in the hospital who started throwing his I.V. stand against the wall. They had all these guys just trying to tape him to the bed. They had to fucking tape him to the bed."

"It almost seemed like it was all acted out, the guy was so outrageous."

"They've gotta do it all with actors, man, otherwise they'd get sued."

"Hey, what's the story with Weasel's car?"

"I tried to start it like three times. Nothin'."

"Such a bummer."

"There's a lot of memories in that car, man."

"Like remember when Weasel was tripping his brains out and wanted to drive it backwards down that hill? You said, 'I'm not up for all this fast driving, man,' and we said, 'Come on, you're going for a cruise.'"

"Weasel was one excellent driver, man."

"Remember when we went to that Foreigner concert, and there was like six of us in the car, and this kid Al D'Angelo had all this Tequila and 'ludes, and like all of a sudden he blows chow all over the windshield, and he was sitting *in the back seat.*"

"No shit!"

"I ain't shittin', man. It got all over fucking everything. Everybody's coats were on the floor. My windbreaker was totally destroyed. It *still* smells like puke."

"Fucking outrageous."

"He didn't give no warning or nothin'. Just all of a sudden he loses his lunch. I never seen anybody puke that *far* before. It was right out of the fucking *Exorcist.* And I was sitting right next to him."

"One time we went over to this guy D'Angelo's house to take him out for a little cruise, because he had all this wicked Hawaiian weed, and Mrs. D'Angelo thought I was fucking retarded. I was tripping, man, but I was totally cool. That lady doesn't know shit. She thought I was mentally deficient. She keeps saying, 'If you won't come in, Alan can't go out.' She kept calling him Alan. So we had to go in and eat some cake or some shit. I practically fucking puked. She kept wanting to know why Al wanted an electric guitar, like maybe it was our idea."

"That lady's insane."

"She makes Al put it to her once a week."

"No fucking shit?"

"That's what Weasel said."

"*Too* intense."

"No wonder Al's so insane."

"One thing I'll say for that guy, he takes a lot of drugs."

"He tried to get Weasel's job, but they wouldn't hire him."

"That was one fucking excellent job, man. You could just get stoned as hell and listen to the radio. I used to go down there and get wasted with Weasel when he was *on the job.* You could just go there and party and watch the fucking gate and nobody gave a fuck."

"Outrageous."

"Too intense."

"You tell me that me and Weasel weren't fucking excellent friends."

"You were, man."

"He used to be a complete weasel. But then he changed."

6
Progress

"Are you finding all your classes?" George Menaro asked me one morning in homeroom.

"I'm doing pretty good," I said. "I still get lost pretty often. Everything looks the same."

"You'll get used to it after a while," George said.

"At my old school," I improvised, "I never could figure out how new kids could get lost. Now I can understand. Things look different when you've been around for a while."

"Yeah, they do," George said. "When I was in tenth I used to get lost all the fucking time."

"One day," I said, "I walked practically around the building looking for my locker, and then it turned out that I was practically standing next to it when I started out."

George said, "Yeah," but I could see that his interest in my problems was not without limits. He drifted away and said something to a friend of his about a baseball game they had both watched on television the night before.

I was beginning to learn what I could talk about and how much I could say without making a complete nuisance of myself.

George was friendlier if I waited to speak until he spoke to me, and if I didn't volunteer too much information. He wasn't a big talker himself, and any warmth he showed me cooled considerably if I seemed to be presuming too much. I was just a new kid, he made it clear, some poor asshole who didn't know his way around.

Relationships among teenagers are founded on awkwardness more than most of them realize. When a typical high school student looks around at his classmates, he sees little but coolness and confidence, people who fit in better than he does. That was certainly the way I thought of my old high school classmates much of the time; no matter how well adjusted I happened to feel at any particular moment, other people seemed to be doing better. At Bingham, though, I saw another picture. Everyone seemed so *shy*. The kids hadn't learned the nearly unconscious social habits that adults use constantly to ease their way through the world. When kids bumped into each other in the halls, they almost never uttered the little automatic apologies—"Oops," "Sorry"—that adults use all the time. They just kept plowing right ahead, pretending they hadn't noticed. One day, when I was hurrying to my history class, I realized I was on a direct collision course with a girl coming the other way. Each of us made a little sidestep, but in the same direction. Just before we bumped, an expression of absolute horror spread across the girl's face. She looked as though she were staring down the barrel of a gun. The bubble of coolness had been burst. She probably brooded about it for the rest of the day.

Well, maybe not. But *I* certainly brooded about it. Being an adolescent is a full-time job, an all-out war against the appearance of awkwardness. No one is more attentive to nuance than a seventeen-year-old. I found myself mulling over the implications of tossed-off remarks for hours at a time. I had an advantage over most of the other kids in knowing that everybody makes little social gaffes at one time or another, and that bad days are inevitably followed by good ones. But that didn't always help. Much of the time I found myself reacting like the other kids, most of whom hadn't learned to take a "long view" of their lives. When a kid in my class came to school one day in a funny-looking pair of shoes that one of his friends eventually laughed at, I could see by his face that he was thinking, Well, that does it, there goes the rest of my life.

On the other hand, I also saw a lot of kindness, mostly in areas of particular local concern. Pimples, for example. One day a classmate came to school with traces of a strange orange acne medication all over his face. I braced myself for what seemed his inevitable humiliation, but no one said a word. The feeling, apparently, was that this could happen to anybody. Even so, it's terrible to have to go to school with something about you that's even just a little bit out of the normal range—with a big red zit on the end of your nose, or an article of clothing that no one else in the history of the world has ever worn.

A lot of the most debilitating awkwardness at Bingham showed up in the relationships between boys and girls. At the beginning of the year especially, boys and girls almost never ate at the same tables in the cafeteria. Boy table, girl table, boy table, girl table. If the sexes had been separated at lunchtime by administrative fiat, the division couldn't have been much more complete. Lunchtime for a lot of the kids actually seemed to be a relief from coeducation, a chance to back away from the idea of sex altogether.

Same-sex relationships had their own complications. Striking up friendly conversations with total strangers was virtually out of the question for most of the kids. The boys in particular kept their distance; any lapse of coolness was a sign of weakness. The girls were more outgoing, but even their amiability had limits. They would cluster around a new girl, especially if she was pretty, but these friendly forays were mostly fact-finding missions. And once the girls had sized up the newcomer, most of them backed off.

The high school reminiscences of a number of people I know are revealing, and suspiciously similar:

"I moved around with a pretty fast crowd, but I was mostly on the fringes of it."

"I wasn't popular in the way that, say, the captain of the football team was, but I wasn't unpopular either. I was friendly with a lot of different kinds of people. I wasn't really in any particular group, but I got along well with people in several of them. Sometimes I'd screw around with the guys who ran the paper and the student council, and sometimes with the kids who did nothing but make A's."

"I was kind of a loner or a drifter in the sense that I didn't belong to a real, exclusive clique. I drifted around in a couple of different circles."

High school students just naturally assume that their friends are better adjusted than they are themselves. Even people I know who really did head high school cliques—people who had actual *followers*—tend to remember themselves as having been aloof. Most teenagers simply haven't seen enough of human nature to understand the defenses their friends put up, and so they imagine their own problems are worse than they are.

The one word that best describes my feelings during my first days at Bingbam is probably "embarrassment." I had to learn to be on guard, and I always seemed to be doing something wrong. It took me most of a day to remember that high school boys almost never cross their legs. Figure it'll crush their nuts, or make it look as though their nuts aren't big enough to crush. Every time I realized that my right calf was sitting on top of my left knee—or, worse, that my thighs were touching—I nearly pulled a muscle trying to get uncrossed before somebody noticed. More than almost anything, a high school boy dreads seeing that bowel-shattering look on a classmate's face that translates ". . . homo?"

Oddly enough, homophobia was more conspicuous among the girls than among the boys. "Auugh!" I heard one girl shouting in the hall. "Sally Mason tried to look at me in the lav!" Girls who seemed just a little bit odd were frequent objects of derision. The reason for this may be that the girls were actually *less* anxious about homosexuality than the boys were. "Lesbian" was just a handy word to throw around if you were mad at someone and wanted to make a public show of it. Among the boys, such words were better left unuttered.

My real embarrassments during those first days were more mundane, however. During the first week, Mr. Amberson, my homeroom teacher, handed out financial aid forms to all of us and told us to take them home and have our parents fill them out immediately. I took mine home, filled it out, asked Ann to forge a parental signature, and brought it back the next day. Mr. Amberson said, "Okay, who's got their financial aid forms?" I handed him mine, then looked behind me. No one else had remembered. Either that, or everybody had remembered but decided not to comply. Day followed day. No other forms materialized. I felt like the king of the assholes.

I consoled myself with the thought that, as an imposter, I couldn't afford to bring myself to the attention of the administration. Anxieties about getting caught were with me always in those first days. Every time a classroom intercom buzzed, I was certain it was the principal calling to ask that I be sent down for a little chat. Sometimes students were paged between classes over the public address system, and I kept imagining I heard my name. When teachers looked at me askance, I trembled.

Despite the fears and the nervous moments, though, I was beginning to be assimilated. I knew more and more names and more and more faces, and I began to be included in more and more conversations. Amy Kendris, an extremely nice girl who sat in the desk in front of mine in math, talked to me every day and was interested in knowing where I had come from and how I was getting along. One afternoon, leaving school, I heard a car honk and turned to look. Much to my surprise, a couple of kids were waving. They didn't stop to offer a ride, but the wave was a genuine boost. Another boost came at lunch one day. I hadn't found anyone to sit with and so had carried my tray to an empty table, figuring I would eat alone. A couple of minutes later, Les Zulinski and Frank Beauchamp came over and set their trays down next to mine. *They* had wanted to sit with *me*. I had difficulty believing it.

Once or twice I worried that I was becoming *too* assimilated, that in some ways I was beginning to think and act too much like a teenager. In the food line one day I was standing behind a small boy who was waiting for one of the kitchen ladies to bring him something they had temporarily run out of. Meanwhile, he was in my way, and I asked him if he would step aside for a second so I could get my dessert. He said nothing and stayed where he was. I tapped him on the shoulder and again asked him to move, but he had decided to play tough. So I laughed and reached over his head, which was at about the level of my breast bone and took my dessert from the shelf above the counter. This was quite cutting. He wilted and stepped aside, but too late. I had humiliated him and I felt bad about it. But I also felt a little exhilarated.

At home, my transformation into a teenager was causing other problems. Ann started a new job about the same time my school year began, so we were both on hectic schedules. I was out of the house by five in the morning and didn't get home till after six at night. By ten I was exhausted. Sometimes it seemed that all Ann and I did together was eat and sleep. There was some excitement in it for me, since every day was an adventure, more or less, but Ann was having a pretty dull time of it. Being married to a high school student is no barrel of laughs.

"Stop acting like a seventeen-year-old," she told me more than once. I had bought new glasses to wear at school, since the ones I normally wear didn't look right, and after a while I took to wearing them at home, too. This did not sit well with Ann. The new glasses just didn't look like *me*. Then I stopped changing my clothes when I got home. At first I had made a point of at least putting on a different shirt, but after a while Ann would come home from a long day at the office and there I would be, stretched out on the couch with the TV on, wearing my aviator glasses and my Led Zeppelin T-shirt and my horrible running shoes. She held up much better than I would have, I am certain. But once, when we were running out to grab some dinner, she stopped me at the door and said, "Take off those shoes."

I wasn't making very scintillating dinner conversation, either. Ann would tell me about something interesting that had happened at work that day, and then I would say something like, "In psychology today this guy I know cut a really tremendous fart. It was incredible!" Not the sort of husband you brag about to relatives.

Through it all, though, Ann was helpful and forgiving. She listened patiently when I told her about whether we had won or lost in gym, or when I complained about a teacher, or when I needed advice about what to do with a medical questionnaire. She also told me stories about her own high school experience and helped interpret the sometimes inscrutable behavior of the girls in my class. She was, in short, a regular mom of a wife.

My other substitute mom, Julia, called from time to time to see how I was doing.

"Are you meeting any girls?" she would ask.

"Well, yes, I guess."

"Do any of them have a crush on you?"

"I don't know. Maybe."

"Maybe?"

"Well, there's this one girl, the one who asked me my name the first day . . ."

"And?"

"Well, her name is Susan Mattey."

"And?"

"Well, she sits next to me in psychology . . ."

"And?"

"Well, she always wants to *talk*."

"My son!"

My real mom called a lot, too, and her letters kept me posted on what her other seventeen-year-old son was up to. She also reminded me of some things I used to do that it had taken me years to forget. It was really wonderful, all the attention I got. With the three of the greatest moms in the world, a guy couldn't help but make some progress.

7
～Real Progress

"I've fallen down on my work at school and don't get along too well with my instructors."

The speaker is a troubled young man in a movie we are watching in psychology. He has gone to visit his family doctor because he believes he has developed a dangerous heart condition. His symptoms are certainly disturbing. In tense situations he suffers pains in his chest, and his heart sometimes beats so vigorously that the sound of it keeps him awake at night. He is anxious and overwrought. His grades are taking a beating. His social life is a shambles. The doctor examines him thoroughly but can find nothing physically wrong. The name of this movie is *Emotional Health*. It was made in 1947. If Coach Chapin had any say in the matter, it would be given an Academy Award.

The doctor scratches his head thoughtfully and delivers his professional opinion.

"I'm going to refer you to a psychiatrist," he says.

The young man is mortified. "Gee, Doc," he protests, "I'm not crazy."

"No," the doctor says, "you're not. And you never will be. *You don't have to be crazy to go to a psychiatrist.*"

From his perch on the desk top at the back of the classroom, Coach Chapin chuckles contentedly. Never mind that our print of this thirty-plus-year-old film is so worn and anemic that it casts a barely visible image on the screen. "This movie puts the whole course in a nutshell," the Coach told us earlier in the period. "It goes right to the heart of *psychology.*"

Coach Chapin shows so many movies in his various courses that he has a gray standard-issue 16-millimeter projector in his classroom on permanent loan from the audiovisual department. Most of the other teachers have to submit equipment requisitions up to a week in advance when they want to show films, but the Coach is ready to roll at any time. Almost every week a messenger from the main office arrives at his door with another armload of the vintage films the Coach orders by the dozen from the educational archives of a local university. The round metal cannisters pile up on his desk and on the rolling stand of the projector. When we run out of things to say in class, or when we come to a chapter in our book for which a movie would provide a handy illustration, the Coach slaps another reel onto his machine and shuts off the overhead lights. There is something so darkly satisfying about watching a movie in a classroom—it's like reading a comic book in church—that I get excited every time the Coach rolls out the projector.

Back on the screen now, the troubled young man in *Emotional Health* is meeting with the psychiatrist his family doctor has recommended. Their conversation has begun to touch upon personal matters, and the psychiatrist asks his patient to tell him about his family.

"Dad works pretty hard," the young man says. "I guess we're not too close."

"How about your mother?" the psychiatrist probes.

The young man hesitates. "I'm much closer to her," he says.

Coach Chapin raises his index finger, smiles, and says, "Aha."

Another of the Coach's favorites is a movie called *Problem Boy*, which he showed us the first week of school. Made in the early 1950s, *Problem Boy* is about a little boy named Tommy who is having serious trouble in elementary school. One day, when the other children have gone to the playground for recess, Tommy spies his teacher's purse lying open on her desk. He reaches inside and pulls out a dollar bill, which he is still holding when the teacher unexpectedly returns to the room. She sees him and stalks toward him, her hands held menacingly in front of her, like claws. The scene cuts to the office of the principal, who is placing a call to Tommy's mother.

"Is he all right?" Mrs. Tommy asks, expecting the worst. The principal reassures her. "Thank God," she says, overprotectively.

But the principal's news is not good. Tommy has been caught trying to steal. In fact, the principal says, now that he thinks about it, "there have been some things missing around the school lately."

Tommy's mother is absolutely shocked. But the principal doesn't want to punish Tommy. "Are you familiar with the counseling center on Pine Street?" he asks.

As Tommy begins to make regular visits to a psychiatrist, we learn more about his family. One night Tommy's father, who has just come home from a long day at the office, puts down the newspaper he is reading and says to his wife, "I spoke with Tomkins today."

Tommy's mother gets up abruptly and leaves the room. "If you want to talk to me," she snaps, "you'll just have to come into the kitchen. I'm not going to shout at you," she lies.

The father tags along docilely and repeats what he has just said. Tomkins has offered him a promotion, but in order to get it he will have to move the family to New York.

His wife stares at him coldly. "Well," she says, "I hope you weren't foolish enough to say yes, were you?"

Tommy's father looks down sadly and mumbles, "I told him I'd think it over." Tommy's mother launches into a long tirade about how stupid such a move would be. They have a nice house they've worked hard for, and so forth. At last Tommy's father, thoroughly defeated, trudges back to the living room with his paper.

Tommy's mother's mother, who lives with the family and has overheard this discussion, marches into the kitchen. "Well," she says, "what have you been making a mess of now?"

When the movie ended, the Coach quizzed us on its message "Who's the problem?" he asked.

My classmates, timidly, offered several interpretations:

"The mother."

"The boy."

"The father."

"The grandmother."

"The teacher."

Coach Chapin chuckled. "The whole bunch, eh? They're all pretty messed up, aren't they?"

We nodded.

"How about that jelly-spined poor excuse for a father?" the Coach continued. "What about him? If I was him, I'd grab the old bag by the scruff of her neck and toss her out the door."

Of course, we do more in psychology than just look at movies. Sometimes the Coach lectures us on the material in our book.

"What it all boils down to," he told us early in the course, "is that the hypnotizer gets you to narrow down your attention span, and once they have you there they can get you to go on an elevator, ride to the eighth floor, and get off—and you'll do it.

You won't have any choice. However, they can't get you to do something against your superego or what is called your moral values. If they told you to kill a person, you wouldn't do it. Otherwise people would go around hypnotizing people to do whatever they wanted them to. I might go down to the bank and hypnotize everybody that went in to bring out all their money to me. Or I could go over to one of these singles bars and hypnotize all the pretty young ladies to come for a picnic, heh-heh, if you know what I mean. I'll admit that it's a little confusing in the book."

The book devotes a disproportionately large number of pages to hypnotism in an early chapter. The authors probably felt the subject would have a magical appeal to young people and make them converts to the science of psychology. My classmates' reaction was tepid, however. Hypnosis doesn't hold a candle to the stuff you can do with computer brain implants and deadly mind-distorting drugs. But the Coach was certainly fascinated. Leaving the textbook altogether, he elaborated on the theme he had been developing:

"It's against the law just to indiscriminately hypnotize people. Why? Because they might tell you something that you aren't supposed to know. The only people allowed to are entertainers. That's because they always have an audience there, but they can't do it on the side."

The psychiatrist in *Emotional Health* would probably be allowed to use hypnosis in his treatment of the troubled young man, but so far he hasn't had to: His patient is telling him plenty without it. After a couple of sessions the doctor has succeeded in tracing the young man's problem back to a grade school teacher who gave him a hard time one day in class. *Problem Boy*, it occurs to me, may owe an inspirational debt to *Emotional Health*. But as the story develops, clear differences appear. For one thing, the troubled young man's father is nothing at all like Tommy's jelly-spined old man. In fact, he is a regular tyrant, who punishes his son whenever he fails to live up to his expectations. The young man, at the urging of the psychiatrist, thinks back over his past. He can't remember very many specifics about his father, but he does recall that "every now and then he'd lock me in a closet." This, the psychiatrist hypothesizes, produced resentment in the son.

"I even planned to kill my father and then run away," the young man confesses.

"But you never did," the psychiatrist points out, a note of triumph in his voice.

"No," the young man says. "But I still resent those—*those in authority.*"

Coach Chapin asserts his own authority by quizzing us periodically on the material we have been covering. Because we don't cover the material very swiftly—our average weekly reading assignment is ten or twenty pages—the quizzes are short, usually only one or two questions. The questions always involve various key words our textbook prints in boldfaced type. On quiz days, the Coach hands out little half-sheets of lined paper, on which we write our names and a numerical heading that enables the Coach to keep track of how many quizzes he has given us during the grading period. One day, for instance, he passed out pieces of paper, gave us the numerical heading ("Roman numeral two, Arabian numeral three"), and asked us, "What is a phenomena?"

This was a tough question, and most of my classmates groaned. Although the word was defined in the chapter we were supposed to be reading, most of us hadn't bothered to crack our books. And the trouble with "phenomena" was that you couldn't really guess the meaning just by looking at it, assuming you'd managed to spell it more or less correctly.

"That's too hard," someone complained.

"It's right there in your reading," the Coach said. "In fact, it's on page three."

"Ohhhhhh," said Dawn Lavin.

"Okay," the Coach said. "Because I'm a nice guy, here's a bonus question for all you geniuses."

"Thank God," someone said.

"Now, don't number it, just write 'bonus' next to it. And the question is, What is a theory?"

There were fewer groans this time, because if we missed this one, it wouldn't be counted against us. One girl had a question, though: "How do you spell bonus?"

The rest of us did the best we could and, when we were finished, passed our papers forward. Students sitting near the front can sometimes gain a small advantage for themselves by looking at the answers on the quizzes passed up from behind and then copying the best ones onto their own papers when the Coach isn't looking.

"A phenomena is plural," the Coach explained when all the papers had been handed in, "because you know in Latin instead of adding an *s* they add an *a*."

"How queer," Dawn Lavin said.

"A phenomena, in psychology, is defined as any observable fact or event," the Coach continued. "That's not quite the way we use it in real life. If you were at a baseball game and you saw a guy knock it clear out of the park, you might say, 'What a phenomena!' It means something out of the ordinary. But in psychology it's just anything you can see."

"What's a theory?" someone asked.

"Hey, wait a minute," the Coach said. "You tell me."

Dawn Lavin raised her hand and read the definition from the book: "A theory is a general principle, based on considerable data, proposed as an explanation for what is observed."

"You get an A in reading, Dawn. Now somebody tell me what all that stuff means."

"A theory," a boy said, "is the tendency to explain a phenomena by means of various hypothesis."

This boy, Larry Koszky, begins all definitions with the words "the tendency." Asked to define psychology itself one day, he said, "The tendency to study the science of the behavior of the mind." For a while he used the words "the belief" in the same way ("Anthropomorphism is the belief in the study of anthropology") but he abandoned this, perhaps because it didn't sound as authoritative.

The Coach, meanwhile, was looking for a better answer. He called on Les Zulinski, the quarterback.

Les smiled. "You got me, Coach. What *is* a theory?"

The Coach shook his head. "It's a good thing you call plays better than you answer questions, Les," he said. "Otherwise we'd be in trouble."

"We *are* in trouble," Les said, referring to the fact that the football team had so far lost every game it had played.

Les and the Coach often engage in good-natured running verbal battles, which liven up the class. One day the Coach asked Les a question for which he was unprepared. "Coming to class without reading your assignment," the Coach warned him, "is like going swimming without your bathing trunks."

Les grinned, blushed, and said, "It's been done," which made the girls in the class giggle and squirm in their seats.

Back to the quiz. The Coach crossed his arms thoughtfully and asked, "Have you noticed that our storms have gotten more violent since we put a man on the moon? That's an example of a theory. It's not proved, so it's not a fact. I look at the moon and see blue cheese. Fact or theory?"

"Theory," we all agreed.

"Green," said Les Zulinski.

"What?" asked the Coach.

"The moon is made of green cheese, not blue."

"Green cheese, blue cheese—I don't care if it's made of *red* cheese, but until we know for sure one way or the other, it's just a theory. Like the theory of evolution."

Darwin is a real thorn in the Coach's side. Every time class discussion veers toward a subject which contradicts or seems to contradict the biblical account of Creation, the Coach becomes combative. He is a deeply religious man who recoils from the moral vacuum he senses at the heart of science. He reads our textbook the way he reads the Bible, which is to say he accepts it literally but bolsters his reading when necessary with a little creative interpretation.

Needless to say, the Coach finds most of his students wanting in the spiritual department. The cynicism and hedonism he perceives in the modern teenager run counter to every instinct in his body. And his opinion of the general run of young people is all the lower because for the most part it was formed a decade ago: He acts and speaks as though the school were teeming with hippies. "It's a neat trick if you can tell the boys and the girls apart nowadays," he told us one afternoon in 1979. Most of the girls were wearing skirts or dresses, and one of the boys had had his hair cut so short you could see his scalp from across the room. The sixties must have been traumatic for the Coach.

Even though he thinks we're a bunch of unprincipled hellions, the Coach loves us and most of us feel the same way about him. It's impossible not to like him. Only a few of the brighter students seem to realize how dated the textbook is, and most of the time even they don't care. My Bingham classmates just don't question their teachers the way my old classmates used to. The Coach would probably be surprised if he realized how much the class of 1980 had in common with the good old students he remembers so fondly from twenty years ago, "before all the nonsense." It occurs to me that our textbook isn't so far out of date after all; in some ways the Wallys and Beavers who illustrate its pages must seem less alien to my classmates than they do to me.

The kids in psychology almost always take the Coach at his word, but every now and then a confrontation materializes, as it did last week when class discussion somehow meandered onto the topic of religion. Susan Mattey, my friend from fifth-period study hall and one of the brightest kids in the class, was talking about the Bible and maintaining that a Christian had to take some of the things in it on faith, or think of them as being true only in a symbolic sense. Coach Chapin strongly disagreed.

"There are some things in *religion* that you have to accept on faith," he said. "But not the Bible. The first half is all prophecies and the second half is all the prophecies being proven to be true. It's all proven, genuine, historic fact. The Bible is what all the various religions have in common. Christians, Catholics, Jews, what have you—they all read the same Bible."

"The Romans millions of years ago believed in lots of gods, and now we don't," Susan said, "so how do we know that millions of years from now people won't be laughing at us?"

"The Romans had their *Odyssey* and we have our Bible," the Coach said, "but the *belief* isn't different. They both have one thing in common: the belief in one god. They all have that. The only ones who don't believe in God are the atheists, and *they* are in very sad shape."

"The things in the Bible have never been substantiated," Susan said.

The Coach grew heated. "Well, who was that gentleman that they hung—or didn't hang, crucified? What was that, a hoax?"

"Well, maybe they really crucified somebody, but how do you know it was the son of God? You have to take it on faith."

"It's not based on faith, sweetheart. You're trying to cover up something by using the word faith. The Bible *has* been substantiated, from *A* to *Z*. It's a proven fact. It's history. If you can't reason from that to a belief in a first cause, then you're in pretty sad shape."

"What about Adam and Eve?" Susan asked. "That isn't a proven fact."

The Coach shook his head. "The fact that Christians believe in Creation and the scientists are trying to prove evolution isn't necessarily a contradiction. There are even some scientists among the clergy who believe in evolution. Myself, I don't particularly believe in the theory, but it's possible that man's *body* came from other animals. Maybe God in His wisdom used some kind of evolutionary process to make the body that he placed man's soul in. But the *soul* did not evolve. Maybe what it was was that first the body evolved, and then the new principle of life, which is immortal, could come in during the creation of Adam and Eve. I will remind you that there is no concrete evidence of evolution. It is a *theory*"

Full-scale arguments with the Coach are rare in psychology, but he and Susan lock horns pretty frequently and sometimes other students are drawn in. One day the subject of Watergate came up, and the Coach announced that "the only thing Nixon did wrong was get caught." I was half-expecting most of the kids to agree with him, but they didn't. The argument that followed was lengthy and intense, and although Susan was the most vocal participant, she wasn't the only one.

"The only thing Nixon did wrong," Susan said, "was be a criminal."

"That's a very libelous allegation you're making there, young lady," the Coach said.

"No, it's not," a boy said. "Richard Nixon is a proven criminal."

The Coach was irate. "All right then, what'd he do wrong? Huh? What law did he break? Huh? Let's hear it."

"Oh, come on, Mr. Chapin," Susan said. "He would have been impeached if he hadn't resigned."

"So that's what you think, is it?" the Coach hollered. "Well,

I've got news for you, dearie. The only thing that man is guilty of is being dumb, by handing over the tapes."

Susan whispered something to a girl sitting across from her and giggled.

"So, you think it's pretty funny, do you? Well, I challenge you to tell me one single thing that man did wrong. Huh? Huh?"

Susan wasn't sure what to say, and the other kids didn't know, either. I had been staying out of the discussion on purpose, but after the Coach made his challenge I couldn't restrain myself.

"Nixon authorized the coverup," I said. "He practically planned it. He obstructed justice, he authorized illegal wiretaps, he planned illegal payoffs and bribes, he collected illegal campaign contributions. He filled the White House with criminals. And he conducted an illegal war in Cambodia. That's all I can think of right offhand."

"Wise guy, eh?" the Coach said. "All right then, if Nixon did all those things, why did President Ford give him a full and complete pardon?"

"If Nixon didn't do all those things," I said, "why did he need to be pardoned?"

Just then, very dramatically, the bell rang. Susan patted me on the back on our way out of the classroom. The next day the Coach flunked both of us on a quiz, even though I think we had the answers mostly right. Susan asked why he hadn't given her any credit.

"Your answers were wrong," he said.

"No, they weren't," Susan said.

"Then they were incomplete."

"No, they weren't."

"Then maybe I just don't like you."

"Maybe so."

"Yeah, maybe so."

The Coach has lots of opinions on subjects that aren't quite so volatile as evolution or Watergate, and frequently he shares them with us:

On injustice: "One of my college roommates was blind. And he got better grades than I did."

On the sixties: "I know a teacher who brought a can of Right Guard to school one day and went around the room spraying it where it was needed."

On the energy crisis. "I think we better put back the death penalty and start choppin' a few of these guys off. I tell you, if they'd reinstate the electric chair, I'd pay the electrical bill."

On the golden past: "You kids don't know anything. We had poor people and retards in my generation."

On cultural history: "Walt Disney was the greatest artistic thinker of the nineteenth century. What an amazing mind. The things he thought of—Dopey, Bashful. Snow White and the Seven Dwarves. The Wizard of Oz."

On the Equal Rights Amendment: "The prom is the high point of a girl's academic career as well as of her social life."

On mental measurement: "They used to have a machine over at the YMCA that would ask you questions in certain fields, like sports, and then give you your IQ."

On genetic engineering: "There's another reason to refute Hitler's theory of a master race. *Mutations.* Let's take the case of interracial marriage. The couple is going to say they don't care about what anyone thinks, and so maybe the kid looks normal, but there's no guarantee that in a few generations, or maybe even in fifty generations, someone's going to have a baby that's going to make them think, Hmmm, I wonder what Grandma *really* looked like."

On the Dionne Quintuplets: "You know, those five girls who were identical twins."

More on Adam and Eve: "The wife came home the other day with a new one. She said, 'God did a pretty good job when He made man, but man was only the rough draft. The real masterpiece was woman.' I coulda belted her."

On conditioning: "Pavlov rang the bell all day long, but it didn't do the dog a bit of good, until they put some food underneath it and he began to drool. He learned to respond to a stimulus, or stimuli, as they sometimes call it."

The Coach made this last observation one day when we had been reading about Pavlov and classical conditioning. In order to demonstrate the principle more clearly, the Coach decided to perform a little experiment. He asked for a volunteer. Les Zulinski raised his hand.

"I'd follow you to the end of the earth," Les said.

"All right," the Coach said. "We're going to teach Les to respond to a stimuli which does not ordinarily bring about a response, but Les will learn because it will be combined with a stimuli that *does* bring it about."

The Coach went over to his big storage closet and pulled out a contraption the size of a shoebox. "One of my old students made this." He chuckled. The contraption consisted of a light bulb, a bell, a large metal bolt, a battery, a throw switch, and some wire, all mounted on a foot-long piece of pine. The Coach told Les to take a hold of the bolt, which he said was an electrode. The Coach threw the main switch to the left, which rang the bell. Les jumped, and let go of the bolt.

"Scared ya, eh?" the Coach said. "Now, pick up the bolt again."

Les did as he was told. The Coach threw the switch again, but this time to the right, which sent the current through the bolt. Les received a mild electric shock and jumped again. Then the Coach threw the switch back to the left and rang the bell again. Les didn't let go of the bolt this time, because he could see what was coming. Then the Coach threw the electrical switch to the right, but before he could get the current on, Les had let go.

"Les has been conditioned," the Coach said triumphantly. "He learned to respond to the bell after it was combined with an electrical shock."

That demonstration went over a few heads, as the Coach's lectures occasionally do. Sometimes it's easier just to sit back and watch the movie—especially now, as *Emotional Health* is building inexorably toward its conclusion.

Up on the screen, the troubled young man and his psychiatrist are far along in their treatment program. "I can see now," the young man says, "that there's no real cause for my resentments. But how will I get rid of them?"

Acknowledging an emotional problem, the psychiatrist explains, is tantamount to curing it. After a few more visits, the young man is back on his feet, with a normal heart rate and an optimistic outlook.

"Can I go now?" he asks the psychiatrist at the end of what proves to be his final visit. "I have a date."

The doctor smiles. "A date—or an *appointment?*"

The young man beams. "A date."

The doctor turns to the camera. "Now that's *real* progress!"

Part Two

October

I am sorry indeed that I have no Greek, but I
would be sorrier still if I were dead.
—R. L. Stevenson

8
ℰBurningGoobers

Before you can burn a goober, you have to hang one. You have to reach down into the toes of your lungs and dredge up a chunk of phlegm the size of a baby Blue Point, and then you have to roll it around on the top of your tongue until you've severed the cable of mucus that wants to snap it back down to your solar plexus, and then you have to launch it, with a single, concentrated blast of nicotine breath, all the way up to the ceiling.

This is no mean feat. To get a goober to hang right, you've got to launch it just so, and on a trajectory that is more or less vertical. If you spit too hard or at too flat an angle, the tail of the goober will slap up against the acoustical tile and the whole thing will flatten into a ugly amber smudge. A properly hung goober will dangle one, two, maybe even three inches from the surface of the ceiling and then gel into a quivering stalactite. If you leave it alone for a couple of weeks, or a couple of years, the stalactite will turn as hard as a piece of quartz.

It would be a crime, though, to let a perfectly usable goober hang from the acoustical tile in the boys' lavatory until it hardened into quartz. That wouldn't take any balls at all. What would take balls would be to climb up onto the toilet bowl or the sink or the radiator by the window and hold your butane lighter, with the valve all the way open, right under the goober until you'd burned it and the ceiling around it as black as a piece of charcoal. The reason that would take balls is that at any moment your teacher or a proctor or even the principal himself might come strolling in on lavatory patrol. And there you would be, standing on public property, apparently trying to set fire to the ceiling of the john. That's the kind of thing you get expelled for. That's the kind of thing they call the *cops* for.

According to Jim Devaney, a pint-sized senior in a black leather jacket with a mouth full of what may be baby teeth, only one person in the history of Bingham High School has ever been expelled for burning a goober: his brother. "Actually," Jim says, "he only got suspended, but it was almost for a month." Jim and I are sitting on the front steps of the high school building, smoking cigarettes before school. I had never met Jim before, but when I offered him a Marlboro he sat down on the next step. "I left my smokes and my lighter at home," he said. "It's a fucking excellent lighter, too." He lit the cigarette I gave him off the one that I was smoking and in doing so knocked off my ember. Now we are smoking in silence, watching the other students arrive.

I shouldn't be smoking at all—I supposedly quit, along with my wife, just over a year ago—but I have lapses every once in a while, and now my "research" has given me an excuse to make up for lost time. When I had my first cigarette this morning, I hadn't had a puff in more than a month, and it made me feel light-headed in a sneaky, ninth-grade sort of way. I even stuttered a little when I asked the girl at the drugstore for my hard pack of Marlboros. My big worry is that tonight when I go home Ann will sniff me out and give me a lecture.

Smoking cigarettes on the front steps is a time-honored tradition among the rougher element at Bingham. Kids who under ordinary circumstances might not be expected to come to school at all set their alarm clocks fifteen or even thirty minutes early to be sure they'll have enough time for a couple of butts. Unlike a lot of high schools, including my old one, Bingham has no indoor or outdoor area set aside for students who smoke. Before and after school are the only times when we are allowed to smoke on school grounds. At one time, a long, dark passageway connecting the main part of the building with a narrow, high-ceilinged structure known as the Vocational Training Wing was used by students as an illicit smoking lounge. Eventually, though, the principal cracked down. The doors at either end of the passageway are now chained and padlocked, and all of the windows are boarded up. As a result there is now no indoor route from the main part of the building to the Vocational Training Wing. Students studying auto mechanics and metal shop have to cross a small central courtyard in order to go to and from their classes. And the only place inside the building where a student can smoke with any degree of safety whatsoever is in one of the lavatories.

Even there, of course, the dangers are considerable. Bingham's teachers sometimes spend their free periods making surprise inspections of the bathrooms. Some teachers even station themselves inside the lavatories during the three-minute breaks between classes. It is not clear whether these sentries are following a confidential directive of the principal or merely acting on their own authority. Whatever the case, their task is made simpler by the fact that the toilet stalls in Bingham's lavatories are all doorless.

Jim spots a daddy longlegs on the railing beside the steps and picks it up. He says, "I'll put it on a chick's head." Instead, he crosses the steps and plants it in the hair of a powerful-looking friend of his who is sitting on a low wall a few feet away. The powerful-looking friend is the spitting image of Jim, but fifteen sizes bigger. An hour and thirty minutes into his day, he could use a second shave. He sits utterly unperturbed for half a minute or so, while the spider jumps from his head to his shoulder and from his shoulder to the ground. When it lands on the pavement at his feet he rouses himself from his morning funk long enough to crush it beneath an immense black motorcycle boot.

"My brother eats 'em," Jim tells me, referring to the daddy longlegs.

"No kidding?"

"Yeah. For five bucks. He'll do anything for money. He'll jump off the bridge on Main Street for five bucks. Six guys gave him five bucks to do that so he made thirty bucks for just jumping off the fucking bridge. He'd do *anything* for money. He'd climb that flagpole over there and take the bird for ten bucks."

"Shit," another boys says. "I'd do it for five."

"My brother would take that light up there for nothin' and put it in his room. He's got one of every kind of street sign. He's got one that says DIP."

The powerful-looking friend lifts his head. "How come your brother's such a hard ass and you ain't nothin' but a faggot?"

"Fuck you."

Generally speaking, there are two kinds of hoods at Bingham High School: Those who are considerably smaller than the rest of their classmates, like Jim Devaney, and those who are considerably larger, like Jim's friend, whose name I never learned. The large hoods tolerate the small ones with the same self-serving indifference that sharks extend to sucker fish. They have a symbiotic relationship founded on the unequal distribution of hormones. Looking at the two groups together, or at any group of adolescents, it is hard to believe that a student's place in the society of his peers is determined by anything more complicated than physical appearance. Ductless glands are everything.

Jim's glands, sadly, have let him down. His formidable black leather jacket is several sizes too big for him: The shoulder seams drop almost a third of the way down his upper arms. The coat looks like a cast-off from one of his larger and more intimidating friends. The label on the back of his new Levi's says that his waist is 27 inches around and that his legs are 28 inches long. Somehow he looks even smaller. His face resembles a ten-year-old's, notwithstanding a wispy mustache that is all but invisible from certain angles. His boots are smaller versions of the black leather monsters his friend is wearing. They have inch-and-a-half heels and round silver buckles. His fingers are thin and nervous. As he smokes, he flicks constantly at the filter of his cigarette with his thumb, occasionally dislodging the ember. He draws the smoke shallowly into his lungs and exhales it in rapid bursts. His head is constantly moving. Every few seconds, he glances over his shoulder to see if anyone is standing behind him or watching him from the building. More than once this morning he has risen suddenly to his feet or changed his position on the step. When a friend of his emerges from a school bus at the curb, Jim hops up and shifts his weight from foot to foot until the friend is near enough to hale. He then sinks back down to the step and begins to pick apart the filter of the cigarette he has just finished.

Survival in a high school for a kid with a 27-inch waist is a pretty tall order. Jim's got to be on his toes every minute of the day. His big friend, on the other hand, can afford to sit quietly and let the world swim into his jaws. For as long as we have been sitting here, he has spoken only once or twice, and, except for the incident with the spider, he has hardly moved. His only regular exertion has been to take the still smoldering butt of each cigarette he finishes and light a new one off the end of it.

The front steps are the most visible place to smoke in the morning, and hence the most prestigious, but there are others.

Senior girls seem to occupy the minor entrances to the right and left of the main one. Black students smoke in a covered entryway adjacent to the faculty parking lot. Younger boys huddle in back of the gym. Younger girls congregate in a corner of the parking lot by the school's rear entrance. Each of these locations is a distinct ecological niche, with its own resident species and its own patterns of behavior, and there is little crossover between them. A few girls regularly venture onto the front steps, and boys frequently roam through the herd of underclass girls in the corner of the parking lot, but for the most part the groups are static.

When I was in junior high and high school, most of my best friends smoked, and the same was true in college. We were never in the majority by any means, but there was always a fair number of us and we represented at least a partial cross section of the class. There were good students and bad students, jocks and nonjocks, partiers and stay-at-homes. The proportion of high school boys who smoke cigarettes has fallen off markedly in the last few years. In 1968, 30.2 percent of male seventeen- and eighteen-year-olds were regular smokers. By 1979 the figure had dropped to 19.3 percent. Only among girls, where sexual emancipation has countered the increasingly urgent warnings of the surgeon general, has cigarette smoking increased. Today the percentage of high school girls who smoke is considerably higher than the percentage of boys who do, having risen from 18.6 percent in 1968 to 26.2 percent in 1979. At Bingham, the girl smokers are not only more numerous, they are also more varied: Whereas the boys who smoke are almost without exception ones who have reputations for being trouble-makers, the girls are more representative. I know several girls who make good grades, take part in a number of extracurricular activities, and smoke heavily.

Girls still have plenty to learn about smoking cigarettes, however. Their first problem is that they will smoke almost anything: Belairs, Eves, Parliaments, Kent Golden Lights,

Saratogas, Benson and Hedges Menthols, Mores, Philip Morris Multi-Filters, Salem Lights. Some of them even change brands every time they buy a pack. It's the kind of thing that drives boys crazy. They just can't figure it out. For a boy, smoking begins and ends with Marlboros. And not just any Marlboros: It's got to be Marlboros in a box, because if you are a teenager there are times when you have to carry your cigarettes in your pants pocket, and if they aren't in a box, they'll get broken.

Another thing that drives boys crazy is the way girls hold their cigarettes—way down at the tips of their fingers—and the way they inhale—as often as not by swallowing the smoke and ejecting it through their nostrils, which isn't really inhaling at all. It's girl inhaling. Girls don't smoke their cigarettes, they nibble at them. Infuriating! And they never smoke them more than about halfway down. If you make a quick survey of the litter on the ground in one of the girls' primary smoking areas, you'll find butts three inches long, which is practically as long as a Marlboro is to begin with.

"Chicks shouldn't smoke," Jim Devaney says. "They shouldn't smoke and they shouldn't drive cars."

Jim has solved one of the problems posed by the smoking ban in an ingenious manner. He has taken an ordinary Bic pen and removed the little blue plastic plug at the end of it. Now, as we sit here, he takes a big drag on his Marlboro, puts his mouth over the end of the pen, and forces the smoke into the cylinder. A thin gray plume jets out of the mysterious little hole in the side of the pen. Jim takes another drag and blows it in, too. A murky brown haze of tar and condensing vapor begins to form on the inside of the cylinder. He forces a few more mouthfuls of smoke into his pen, and then urges me to try the same thing with mine, which I do, reluctantly.

"This is my Nic pen, man," Jim says. "If I have a nic fit in the middle of the day, I just pull it out and suck on it for a while, and then I'm okay."

I force a few drags through my own pen, and then suck on the end. It tastes, well, terrible. Sucking on a Nic pen is about as pleasant as chewing up an old cigarette butt. But Jim is sold on the idea. After he has finished charging his pen, he shakes it briskly over the wall. A long string of brown saliva slithers into the bushes.

Other kids have other ways of coping with the no-smoking rule. Some of them carry cigarettes behind their ears all day, pulling them out from time to time for an unlit drag. Others open their Marlboro boxes on the sly and take a big whiff between classes. You do what you can. And at the end of the day, as often as not, you stick a fresh cigarette in your mouth when you get your coat out of your locker, and you light it with your butane lighter the exact instant you set foot outside, if not a second or two before.

Most of the kids who smoke linger in the yard of the building for a few minutes after school to enjoy one last cigarette on school property. Some of the kids aren't allowed to smoke at home, so for them this may be the last cigarette of the day, at least the last leisurely one. They stand around the bases of the maple trees, or hang out on the steps, or sit on the low stone wall. Sometimes they are joined by others, including a girl who ought to have been a member of the class of 1980 but who dropped out last spring to have a baby. The baby's father is a senior at another school. Several days a week the mother walks over to Bingham from her parents' house a few blocks away, pushing her baby in a stroller. She waits for school to let out, then joins a couple of her old classmates on the wall for a few cigarettes. Before she sits down, she parks the stroller front-first against a wall a few feet down the sidewalk, so her baby won't roll away.

Now the warning bell rings, which means we have three minutes to get ourselves to homeroom and be counted present.

Jim Devaney stubs out his cigarette and plants his Nic pen in his mouth.

"Maybe I'll see ya later in the lav," he says, and we both go inside.

9
ᏉJournalism

"You need an activity," Ann told me one evening at dinner.

"An activity?"

"Something to keep you out of trouble at school."

"What do you mean?"

"Stamp club, biology team, I don't know. Male cheerleading. Instead of spitting on the ceiling in the bathroom."

"*I* never did that," I protested. "That was just a friend of a friend."

"And what was that in your pocket when you came home tonight?"

"What? You mean my wallet?"

"Cigarettes."

"Oh, Christ."

"If you're going to smoke," she said, "you can do it in front of me. You don't have to sneak around."

Ann was right, about the activity, anyway. I had been thinking, during the first weeks of school, that I needed to get involved in something that would give me an opportunity to meet more students. Schedules at Bingham are so tightly structured that there isn't much time for a stranger to make friends. Other new kids were having trouble, too: I heard a girl in my psychology class complaining to Susan Mattey that in her three weeks at Bingham she hadn't made a single friend. Susan was vaguely sympathetic, but not much more, and since then the two of them hadn't exchanged another word. I felt a little guilty that I seemed to be doing better than this genuine newcomer was. After all, I knew Susan, and I was on fairly good terms with a number of other students, including George Menaro and his friends. In gym I knew Les and Frank quite well, and the three of us ate lunch together almost every Tuesday and Thursday. I had been taking advantage of my newness to get to know kids I might not be able to talk to later, kids like Jim Devaney. But now I needed something more. So I decided to try out for the newspaper.

Before I went to Bingham, one of the issues that had troubled me most was how involved in the workings of the school I could in good conscience allow myself to become. I decided never to join a group if my participation would cause a legitimate student to be excluded. This ruled out such possibly interesting activities as trying out for a play or a team, or becoming involved in a student club with limited membership. For some of the same reasons, I had thought it would be best to avoid the school's publications. But as time went by the newspaper began to seem like my best bet. I wouldn't try to be an important member of the staff, I decided; I'd just be another part of the deadwood, and never take on a big assignment, and never fill space that another kid might be interested in. But first I had to get on the staff.

As is true at virtually all high schools, Bingham's newspaper is an adjunct of the journalism class. The kids who make up the staff receive grades for the stories they write and the photographs they take. I didn't actually want to become a graded member of the class, since that would have made it impossible to sit on the sidelines, but I thought it might be possible to join the class on a noncredit basis.

The Bingham High School *Bomber* is put together in a room called the Publications Office, which is around the corner from my homeroom. It is a small room filled with typewriters and light tables, and it is right next door to Room B-31, which is the journalism classroom. In the outer wall of the Publications Office is a huge plate-glass window, designed to let teachers and administrators keep an eye on unsupervised activities within. For some time I had seen kids working in the office, and one day after school at the end of September, I went inside.

There was a girl at one of the tables staring at a blank sheet of paper she had rolled into her typewriter.

"Hi," I said. "I was wondering if you have to be in journalism to work on the paper."

"I don't think so," she said. "But you'll have to ask Mrs. Griswold."

"Is she the teacher?"

"Yeah," the girl said. "She's the adviser. She's probably next door."

I thanked her and left. Through the window I saw her pull the still-blank piece of paper out of the machine and wad it up, then roll in a new sheet.

Mrs. Griswold was standing at her desk, going over an article with the boy who had written it.

"Look at this," she said to the boy. "This is supposed to be an article about the guidance counselors, but you don't even mention who they are. You don't even mention what they *do*."

"I never talked to them," the boy explained.

"You never talked to them?"

"They were always busy and then I was going to but somebody had the tape recorder."

"So you just winged it?"

"Yeah, sort of. Come on, Mrs. Griswold, this is the most boring story in the world."

Mrs. Griswold noticed me standing in the door and asked me what I wanted. I introduced myself and told her I wanted to work on the paper. She nodded.

"It all depends on what your schedule's like," she said. "We do almost all our work on the paper during class time fifth and sixth periods. Are you free either of those?"

"I've got class sixth," I said, "but I have study hall three days a week during fifth."

"Did you write for the paper at your old school?"

"Yeah," I said, "a little."

"Well, then," she said, "why don't you bring in a sample of your writing and then we'll see."

That night at home I sorted through some of my old high school newspapers, looking for something I could hand in. I had been editor of the paper, and most of the things I had written were too long to pass for the work of an underling. Either that or they were hopelessly outdated, like a short article on a citywide anti-Vietnam rally. I finally picked out a brief item written by someone else about the retiring athletic director, and then reworked it into late-seventies studentese.

"Mr. C——," my version began, "is retiring as athletic director of the school. He has been athletic director of the school since 1955, when he first came here. When interviewing people about Mr. C—— nothing other than high respect and praise were mentioned. Mr. R—— the varsity basketball coach summed up people's feelings. He said 'Mr. C—— is always pleasant, easy to work with, and above all never gets upset. He has been a fully devoted athletic director.'"

I threw in a few misspellings and threw out a few commas and the apostrophe, and wrote it all out longhand. The next day I put it on Mrs. Griswold's desk before school.

When I went to check with her later in the day, I was apprehensive. Maybe I had underestimated the writing ability of the *Bomber* staff, and Mrs. Griswold would tell me no, she was sorry, I just wasn't up to snuff. The *Bomber* hadn't published its first issue yet, so I had no basis for comparison. When I knocked on the door of the journalism room my heart was pounding.

"David!" Mrs. Griswold said. "I loved your article! I've talked with Mrs. Wheelock in Guidance and you'll be starting here on Friday!"

So much for underestimating the writing ability of the *Bomber* staff. I was going to have to make a few changes if I meant to keep a low profile. But there was plenty of time to do something about that, and on Friday I signed out of my study hall and put in my first day in journalism.

Mrs. Griswold was a lean, attractive woman in her middle fifties who would have looked right at home on the city desk of a daily newspaper. She treated the kids in her class like real reporters and tried to maintain an atmosphere of boisterous journalistic camaraderie. It was easy to imagine her standing drinks for her staffers in some smoky reporters' dive, keeping the crowd at the bar in stitches with back-room anecdotes about corrupt officials and shady politicians. She wanted the kids to feel like journalists and to function together as a staff, so when I arrived she wasted no time in trying to make me feel at home.

"Shut up for a second," she told the class when I came in. "This is David Owen. He's going to be in here three days a week, ungraded, from now on, and I want you to show him how things work. Bill, Scott, and Eric, you take him to lunch with you when you go and the four of you sit together. Linda, you take him over to the Publications Office and show him where the things are, and then take him down to the darkroom and introduce him to Carl. Carl Morgan's the head photog, Dave. Do you take pictures?"

"No," I said.

"Too bad, but no problem. Okay, now, hop to it."

Linda was Linda Smoley, one of the two coeditors. She was all business. She led me over to the Publications Office and began opening cabinets and drawers.

"You'll find everything you need in here," she said. She gave me a mimeographed sheet that was headed "HOW TO PRE-PARE COPY" and whose first instructions were, "Indent all paragraphs five spaces Do not exceed thirty words per para-graph." I stuffed it into my notebook

"These are the light tables, Dave." Linda said. "You ever see one of those?"

"Yeah," I said. "We had one at my old paper." Then I added, "But I never used it."

"Don't worry. Somebody will show you." She gave me one of the previous year's issues to look at.

"Have you guys put out a paper yet this year?" I asked.

"Naw," she said. "We're a little behind. You can probably get an assignment if you want one."

We went downstairs to the darkroom. Carl Morgan was hanging up long strands of developed film to dry in the outer room.

"Glad to meet you " Carl said. "You new at Bingham?"

I said yes

"Where do you live?" Linda asked.

This was a question I wasn't really prepared for. The address I had used on my transfer papers belonged to an adult friend who lived in Bingham. It was well off the beaten track, and in a neighborhood filled mostly with single people and young fami-lies, but I was worried that one of the kids might know somebody who lived nearby and begin to ask embarrassing questions.

"Over on Lincoln Street," I said, a little hesitantly.

"Never heard of it," Linda said.

"Me either," Carl said. "Where is that?"

Another question I was unprepared for. I had walked between

it and school many times, but I wasn't quite sure where it was in relation to everything else. I figured my best bet was to be vague.

"It's sort of over, well, if you go down Main Street and then turn off toward the highway a couple of blocks . . . well . . ."

"What shopping center is it near?"

"Well, you know the one that's, well, over right by the highway?" They didn't, and I was making it up. "I guess I don't know my way around too well yet," I said.

"Sure, Dave," Linda said. "You're still new."

The kids in journalism were certainly more inquisitive than most of the ones I had met until that time. In fact, their persistence made me nervous. I had never felt more in danger of being found out. And at lunch I got another grilling.

"Where'd you come from, Dave?" Scott asked.

"Kansas City."

"You a Royals fan?"

"Yeah."

"Sorry, pal, the Royals blow."

"Where do you live, Dave?"

"On Lincoln Street," I said. "Way the hell over."

"Never heard of it," Bill said. "Where is it?"

"Well," I said, gesturing mysteriously in the air, "it's sort of over on Main Street, and then you turn off down this other street by this drugstore, and over down this—"

"Forget it, Dave, you're hopeless."

"You see a lot of movies, Dave?"

"Some," I said. "Do you?"

"Sure. What have you seen?"

I tried to think, but my mind was a blank. Finally I remembered *Animal House*.

"Tough movie. What about *Damien*?"

"No."

"*The Amityville Horror*?"

"No."

"*Meatballs?*"

"No."

"*Alien?*"

"No."

"*Dawn of the Dead?*"

"No."

"*Halloween?*"

"No."

"*Life of Brian?*"

"No."

I was beginning to perspire. Fortunately, they ran out of titles.

"Geez, Dave," Scott said. "You haven't seen *anything*."

"Do you have cable TV?"

"No."

"*No?*"

"We just moved."

I was saved when a straggler from the class came into the cafeteria and passed our table.

"Hey, Ed," one of the kids at our table said. "Griswold wants to see you."

"Swear to God?"

"I swear."

The straggler said, "Oh, shit," and left the cafeteria to look for Mrs. Griswold. As soon as he was out of hearing, the guys at the table burst out laughing.

"What a sucker!" Eric said.

"Did you see what I did? I only said *swear,* see? I didn't swear to God."

Pranks like that were big in journalism, and I was in on a lot of them. As time went by, I got to be better and better friends with the guys I met the first day. There was Bill Scalet, the other coeditor, who was the class cutup and was always getting in trouble with Mrs. Griswold; there was Eric Laver, the sports editor, who liked to fool around but always managed to extricate himself before he got yelled at; and there was Scott Murphy, a junior staff member, who went along when the other guys wanted to fool around but got nervous if things started to go wrong.

One day we decided to ditch lunch. It was against the rules to leave school without permission, but sneaking out was fairly easy and a lot of students did it regularly On this particular day, lunch was a vegetarian horror that nobody wanted to eat, so Bill suggested leaving. Eric backed out at the last minute, but Scott and I went along.

We slipped away from the pack near the entrance to the cafeteria and left by a side door. When we had cleared the faculty parking lot, Bill broke into a run. Scott and I tagged along behind and followed him into the parking lot of a Bonanza Steak Pit a couple of blocks away.

"Let's go here," Bill said, panting.

Scott shook his head: "Too expensive."

We ran across the street and another parking lot and went into a Dunkin' Donuts that had a short-order grill. When our hamburgers hadn't appeared after two or three minutes, Bill and Scott began to get nervous.

"I *told* you we should have gone to Bonanza,' Bill said.

"Oh, Jesus," Scott moaned. "There's only twelve minutes left in the lunch period."

"We're fucked!"

The waitress brought our hamburgers but had forgotten my french fries. I wanted to ask her for them, but Scott stopped me.

"Is a lousy french fry worth getting suspended?" he asked.

"We've got plenty of time," I said. "The other guys probably haven't even gotten their trays yet." But Scott held his ground.

The waitress knew Bill by name and refilled his Coke for nothing, but he didn't stay to finish it. We paid our checks, left big tips, and took off at a full run across the parking lot. I was glad I hadn't eaten any french fries after all; a barely chewed hamburger bouncing around in my stomach was all I could handle. We pulled up short of the high school and tried to figure out the best way to get back inside. I suggested going in through the main entrance at a slow walk, on the theory that the more obvious you are about breaking a rule, the less likely you are to get caught. Scott and Bill treated this as an extremely radical proposal ("You ought to have your brains counted," Bill said), but eventually that's what we did.

"Dave, you're a genius," Bill whispered as we sailed past the principal's office.

The other kids were still eating when we got to the cafeteria, so we had time to kill. The entire expedition, including a half-mile run, had taken less than fifteen minutes. Bill belched sonorously when we got back to the classroom. I felt sick for the rest of the day.

Eating in the cafeteria sometimes made Bill and Scott just as nervous as eating at the Dunkin' Donuts. Mrs. Griswold was lax about lunchtime discipline, letting us go to the cafeteria most days without supervision, but when she began to hear unfavorable reports about our behavior in the cafeteria, she decided to crack down.

"From now on," she announced, "you will *not* be late to lunch and you will *not* be late getting back to the classroom. Do I make myself clear?" She singled out Bill and Scott as the worst offenders and accused them of luring Eric and me away from the straight and narrow.

The bawling out lasted about fifteen minutes, and by the time it was over, we were ten minutes late for lunch and certain to be last in line. Bill and Scott were angry at Mrs. Griswold for picking on them in particular, and they were determined to get revenge.

"I don't care what that bitch does," Bill said as we stood in the line. "I'm gonna stay until I've eaten my lunch."

"Me too," Scott said.

"Me too," I said.

"Oh, all right," Eric moaned.

When we finally got our trays and found a table, there were only five minutes left in the period.

"Eat *slow*," Bill said.

"Jesus Christ," Scott said. "We're gonna get *nailed*."

"Just eat slow," Bill said. "If she gets mad at us, we'll just tell her we have a right to eat a decent lunch, and if she's gonna bawl us out during lunch, then that's her tough titty."

At 11:45, the time our group was supposed to leave, Eric picked up his tray and said, "I'm not getting in trouble, man."

"Oh, Christ, Eric," Bill said. "You haven't eaten *half* of your hotdog."

"Tough shit. I'm going back."

Scott moaned. "You're gonna stay, aren't you, Dave?"

"Sure," I said. I took a tiny sip of my chocolate milk, to prove I was with them.

Scott and Bill weren't moved. They were both eating faster now, and talking about all the trouble we were going to get into.

"That fucking Eric!" Bill said. "He's gonna get our asses kicked."

I pointed out to Bill that the table right next to ours was filled with girls from journalism, including Linda Smoley. They were eating at a leisurely pace, talking and laughing.

"Don't worry," I said, "they're staying, too, so if anybody gets in trouble we'll all get in trouble together. And besides, we *won't* get in trouble, because we didn't have time to eat."

"What if they have *permission* to stay late?" Bill said.

"Oh, Jesus!" Scott said. "I never thought of that!"

"We're screwed, we're screwed." Bill was in despair. He called out to the other table, "Hey, Linda, do you guys have permission from Mrs. Griswold to stay late, or what?"

Linda laughed. "What are you talking about? We're just eating our lunch."

"She's lying," Scott whispered. He began to gather up his trash.

Bill pondered deeply, then had a brainstorm. He whispered, "Let's go back now and then see if *they* get in trouble."

Scott said, "Yeah!"

We turned in our trays and practically ran back to class. Eric was the only person in the room.

"Quick!" Bill shouted. "Get the tape recorder. When Griswold gets back we'll tape her bawling out Linda."

Scott put the recorder on the floor in front of Mrs. Griswold's desk and draped a coat over it. He set the microphone behind a book. Bill was in ecstasy.

The tape ran ten minutes before there was anything to record. Mrs. Griswold came in a little after noon, with Linda and the other girls behind her.

"We were late today, people," she said, "but that was my fault. I didn't give you enough time to eat."

And that was that. Bill and Scott were crushed.

Bill had been having a pretty rough time in journalism this year. Even though as coeditor he held a position of real responsibility, sometimes he just liked to screw around. Mrs. Griswold seemed to keep at least one eye on what he was doing.

"Did I ever tell you I used to be a hood?" he asked one day while we were waiting in line in the cafeteria. Bill was small but had the hard, rangy look of a son of a working man. His dad, in fact, worked in one of the big factories on the outskirts of town, in the compound Bill called "Realityville." "He's sort of a foreman, you know," Bill told me. Bill's hair was longer than average—about construction-worker length—and he was culti-vating a thin little mustache that never seemed to be going anywhere. On the evolutionary tree of hooddom, Bill stood several branches above Jim Devaney, but well below Jim's powerful-looking friend.

"I was bad news, man," he said as we edged forward in the line. "I used to get my butt kicked every day by the principal. And up until the sixth grade I made good grades. I was making like A's, but then in junior high school they didn't divide you up by how smart you were, they just put you anywhere they felt like. I was in the class with all these colored guys and retards. All we did was fuck around. We didn't study or nothin'. I didn't learn shit. So I became a hood like everybody else. I used to wash my hair like three times a week, if that."

If it hadn't been for journalism, Bill said, he might still be a hood. Along about tenth grade he discovered he had a knack for writing, and last year Mrs. Griswold promoted him to the top spot over the heads of some likelier candidates. She thought he deserved a break. But Bill's past still had a hold on him. Sometimes he felt he was being pulled in opposite directions. And, as often as not, when he felt the strain, he got himself in trouble.

Even so, Bill told me, there was no possibility of his actually becoming a hood again. High school hoods were just a completely different kind of animal from junior high school hoods. "They're *tough* motherfuckers," he said. "Those guys don't think twice about stomping on you if you get in their way." In fact, Bill's anxieties about hoods were the main reason it was taking us so long to get our lunch. The food line over on the far side of the cafeteria was much shorter, but that line was generally known as the "Hood Line," and Bill didn't want to take chances. Most of the guys in the Hood Line were about six feet tall and a hundred and eighty pounds. They were all wearing leather jackets and seven-pound motorcycle boots. They all had wallets that hooked onto their belts with metal chains. Not exactly the kind of guys you would ask to lend you a dime for chocolate milk.

When we had our trays and had found a place to sit, Bill told me about what had gone on in journalism the day before (when I had been in gym). He said, "Linda Smoley and a few other people were over in the Publications Office, so I went in and said, 'Linda, Mrs. Griswold wants to see you.' She didn't really, but Linda went in and asked what she wanted. She was so pissed off when she came back! So then Scott went in about ten minutes later and says, 'Linda, Mrs. Griswold wants to see you,' and she went again! We did it about five times and she fell for it every time." He leaned back in his chair and laughed. "Yeah," he said, "I used to be a bad ass. Now when I fuck around it's just for laughs. But junior high was where I learned all my *techniques*."

10
❧Futures

My first reporting assignment for the *Bomber* was the article on guidance counselors I had heard being discussed the day I went to see Mrs. Griswold about joining the class. The student to whom it had originally been assigned (Scott, I later realized) wanted nothing more to do with it. By now the story had a "news peg," Mrs. Griswold said; the Guidance Office was putting together a financial-aid conference for the parents of students who were planning to go to college. I was to write my article about that, and confine myself to 150 words.

I took my little notebook down to the Guidance Office and was sent in to speak with Mrs. Collier, the head of the department. She was tiny and gray-haired and reluctant to talk to me.

"You really ought to go talk with the students on the committee," she said. "I'm sure you'll want to put their names in the paper."

"There may not be enough room," I said. "All I really need is a little information about the conference."

She said, "Oh, well," and gave me the details. Then we talked for a little while about scholarships and the cost of education.

"The price of schools these days is so outrageous," she said. "And most of the parents do need help. But you would be surprised how few of them actually have any idea of what is available."

I thanked her for being so helpful and asked if she would spell her name for me.

"Oh, dear," she said. "What do you need my name for?"

"I just want to make sure I have it spelled right."

"But you're not going to put it in your article, are you?" Her face was pale.

"I was going to," I said. "When I quote you I'd like to be able to use your name."

"*Quote me?* Oh, my goodness. What in the world are you going to quote?"

"Oh, I don't know." I flipped through my notes. "Maybe what you said about the price of schools and parents needing help and all. Just to liven it up."

"Oh, heavens," she gasped. "Oh, heavens. You can't quote me on that. I won't allow it! I'll call Mrs. Griswold. If those colleges found out . . . Oh, my! I'm sure they have their reasons for charging what they do, heavens, with inflation and all. Oh, my! There's no telling what might happen."

I was baffled, but tore the page out of my notebook. She sank back into her chair, sighed, and dabbed her cheek with a Kleenex.

I have no idea what horrors Mrs. Collier imagined would befall her if anyone ever learned what she thought of the cost of a college education. Maybe she was afraid some thin-skinned college president would track her down and throttle her in her sleep. "So, you think thirty thousand dollars for a bachelor's degree is out of line, do you, you contemptible old woman?" Whatever the reason, her attitude was typical of the department. Almost all of the kindly old ladies of the Guidance

Office had been educated within a few miles of Bingham; as a consequence they looked upon more distant (and more prestigious) colleges with a certain amount of awe. The tiny library of college catalogs in the Guidance Office was heavily weighted in favor of small local schools and community colleges. The ladies just didn't want to presume or impose. The people who run colleges have enough to worry about without a lot of high school students applying to get in.

A little under two-thirds of Bingham graduates eventually go on to some form of higher education. "Higher education" in this case refers not only to four-year colleges but also to one-, two-, and three-year schools and to vocational training programs in fields like hair-styling and diesel maintenance. Roughly thirty percent of all graduates spend at least one year in a four-year college, and a majority of the schools attended are close enough to Bingham to be referred to as local.

Bingham High School hasn't sent a student to an Ivy League school in three or four years. There are several reasons for this. One, perhaps the most important, is economic: Big-name schools charge big tuitions, and most people can't afford to pay them, even if they get help. Another reason is academic: In 1979 Bingham had only one National Merit Semifinalist. A third reason has to do with the Guidance Office: Bingham students don't get much advice about colleges.

Which is not to say they don't get any. Mrs. Wheelock came to my homeroom one morning to give us some information about Scholastic Aptitude Tests, which most colleges and universities require.

"Applications for SATs are due in six days," she began. "If you want to take the test you'll have to fill out the application and get it in by next week. If you miss the deadline you'll have to wait until the tests are given again a month later." She paused. "Now, how many of you are planning to go to college?" Six or seven of us, out of thirty, raised our hands. "Do you know how to send away for college applications?" Silence. "If you know what fields you are interested in you can come down to the Guidance Office and look through our catalogs for schools that offer the programs you want."

In the middle of Mrs. Wheelock's spiel, the voice of the assistant principal thundered over the public-address system: "May I have the attention of all homerooms please? I have a special announcement for juniors and seniors. All juniors who desire class rings, and all seniors who desire them but did not order them last year, must bring a twenty-dollar deposit *in cash* by Monday."

Remarkably, Mrs. Wheelock kept talking right through the announcement. She was explaining the SAT schedule and saying something about alternate test sites. Just as she asked if there were any questions, the assistant principal read another announcement:

"May I remind all students eligible for the reduced-cost lunch program that you must submit a new application for the program by the end of the day if you wish to receive a weekly lunch card on Monday and on every Monday thereafter. Old applications are no longer valid. End of announcements."

"Thank you, Mr. Amberson," Mrs. Wheelock said, and she breezed out so she could get to the next homeroom on her list before first period began. I realized she had forgotten to mention where a student interested in taking the SAT could find one of those applications that were due in six days. The applications were in the Guidance Office, presumably, but Mrs. Wheelock hadn't said anything about them, and she certainly hadn't brought any with her. Still, her two-minute, mostly unintelligible talk was the only unsolicited college advice I got from the Guidance Office all semester.

Students who were planning to go to college were left essentially on their own, which meant they had to keep track of the numerous deadlines for tests and applications and try to arrive at reasonable decisions about where they wanted to go. Most of the information they had about specific schools came not from the Guidance Office but from commercial guides and from friends. The one service the Guidance Office did provide was to schedule meetings with college representatives. There were usually a couple of these every day during October and November, and most of the college-bound kids went to several. The meetings lasted about thirty minutes and were held either in the Guidance Office or in an empty classroom nearby. Because the meetings were almost always scheduled during class time, a student who wanted to attend one needed to obtain a pass signed by both a guidance counselor and the teacher whose class was being missed. The Guidance Office made these passes freely available, but teachers' signatures were sometimes hard to come by. A few teachers were openly suspicious of any student who wanted to skip class, even if it was to attend a college meeting. When a girl in my English class asked our teacher, Mr. Quennell, if he would sign her pass, he told her, flatly, no.

"That's the oldest trick in the book," he said.

"But, Mr. Quennell, it's for one of the schools I'm applying to."

"Well, then, if you're applying there anyway, you don't need to go to the meeting, do you?"

"I still need to find out if I want to *go* there."

"No. No way. Period."

"But why? Seniors are supposed to be excused for any college meeting they want to go to."

"Not in my class they aren't. We have a vocab quiz that day."

"But those only take about five minutes. Anyway, we all know what the words are going to be beforehand, so what does it matter if I take it at a different time?"

"It matters because I say it does."

"I'll even take it today if you want. I'll come in after school."

"No. End of discussion."

Most teachers were better about letting their students go to college meetings than Mr. Quennell was. I went to two meetings and had no trouble getting out of class for either. At one of the meetings, for a small private college not far from Bingham, I ran into Bill Scalet and Amy Kendris, my friend from math.

Amy was a fairly ordinary-looking girl with short, straight, blond hair. She and Bill had been in school together since kindergarten, and they ran around with more or less the same crowd: Bill's friends from journalism, Amy's friends from her own classes, some other kids they had known since childhood. Now I was a part of that crowd, too, and Amy and I had become pretty good friends. One day, when I had to get back to New York in a hurry, she drove me to a bus station in a neighboring town on her way to her after-school job. I didn't tell her where I was really going; I just said I had to run an errand for my father. She said she didn't mind taking me because she had to go anyway. Most days after school she worked several hours reshelving books in the community college library, and a few nights a week she took classes. She was trying to earn some college credits ahead of time so she would be able to graduate in three years when she finally went away to a *real* school.

Amy thought about college a lot. Almost every day in math she spent free moments thumbing through a book the size of a phone directory that listed all the schools in the country. "I want to go to California," she told me, "because that's just about as far away from Bingham as you can get." Sometimes, when she found what seemed like an interesting school, she would hand the book back to me and ask me what I thought.

Even though she was set on going to California, Amy was also looking at schools a little closer to home, just in case, which was why we ended up at the college meeting together. Bill was there against his wishes. Amy had dragged him along because she thought he was being too cavalier about the entire college question. At the moment, Bill was more or less determined to go straight to work after graduation, but Amy had persuaded him that he couldn't make a rational decision if he didn't at least give college a chance.

"Dave!" Bill said when he saw me in the Guidance Office waiting for the meeting to begin. "What the heck are you doing here?"

"Just going to the meeting," I said.

"You'll never get in, Dave." He turned to Amy. "This guy's a basket case."

"Bill didn't want to come," Amy explained.

"It doesn't matter," I said. "I just saw the admissions guy and he's writing out Bill's rejection by hand, right now, so he can give it to him in person."

"Very funny," Bill said. "Hey, you know what happens at these things, don't you? It's just like the Moonies. You go down to the little meeting in the Guidance Office, and then they tie you up and throw you in the back of a truck."

"Oh, Bill," Amy said.

"And then when you wake up there's all these assholes putting their hands all over you and telling you what a great guy you are. Well, no thanks."

"You just don't have a positive attitude about college," Amy said, "just because your parents and your brother never went."

"Hey," Bill said. "My brother makes fifteen thou a year. He's no slouch. Going to college wouldn't have done a damn thing for him."

"It might have given him a little culture," Amy said.

"Well, excuuuuse me!" Bill said.

Actually, there were times when Bill thought he might end up in college after all. One day, as we were walking home from school, I asked him if he was planning to go.

"I don't know," he said. "Maybe to junior college after a year or two. At least when you're in school you don't have to do anything."

"What do you want to do when you graduate?"

"Oh, shit," he said. "I don't know. I don't know what I *could* do. I'll probably just go to work at the factory or something. Realityville, you know."

"How about journalism? You *are* the editor of the paper."

"I don't know," he said. "Mrs. Griswold is pretty discouraging sometimes. I don't know if I could hack it."

"The world isn't all Mrs. Griswold," I said. "Anyway, if she was really all that great at journalism, she'd be doing it, not teaching it."

Bill laughed. "I never thought of that," he said.

Now, though, at the guidance meeting, Bill wasn't very enthusiastic. "I better not have to say anything," he whispered.

"Why would you have to say anything?" Amy whispered back.

"You just wait," Bill said. "He'll start out by saying something like 'This is a different kind of interview. *You* ask the questions,' and then we'll all have to tell him our hobbies and everything."

The admissions officer finished arranging his paper. "Rather than my giving you a lot of information you don't need," he said, "why don't we start out by having you tell me what fields you think you might be interested in, and then we'll talk about some of those."

Bill laughed so hard he had to put his head down on his desk to keep himself under control. "I have ESP," he whispered.

When Bill and I were called on to speak, we both said we were undecided. Amy said she was interested in computers. "We have numerous terminals and a fine series of courses," the officer said. The other kids all mentioned professions of one sort or another: Three said premed, three business, one accounting, one business or biology (i.e., premed), one prelaw, one education. Nobody mentioned a liberal arts major, like history or English.

"I can see you are by and large quite career-oriented in your aspirations," the officer said. "We are seeing this more and more, of course. Although we have primarily been a liberal arts institution, we are quite responsive to the needs of our students, and I am confident all of you will find the kinds of programs you need to qualify you for the various professions you have mentioned. Business in particular is a popular course of study, and our business administration graduates regularly move on to satisfying jobs and prestigious MBA programs."

A girl named Mary sitting up near the front took copious notes through all of this and interrupted several times to ask questions. "My father went to your school," she said, "and I have a cousin there now, Leslie Mason—do you know her?" The officer chuckled and said no. Mary had another question: "What are the things you want in a student, in order?"

"Well," the officer said, "we have no set formula, but the order is probably something like this: your academic record and class rank, your SAT and Achievement scores, your extracurricular activities and personal accomplishments."

"What about relatives who went there?" Mary asked. "Doesn't that help if you are related to someone?"

"The most important considerations are the ones I just gave you," he said. "I couldn't tell you for a fact that relatives of alumni would be given any kind of special treatment."

"How good do your SAT scores have to be?" a boy asked.

"In general," the officer said, "we are looking for a combined SAT of one thousand, such as five hundred on the verbal and five hundred on the math."

Mary looked perturbed. "But that's just the average, right? You take them a little lower, too, right?"

One theme the officer kept returning to was the proximity of his school to Bingham. "Nowadays," he said, "most people can't afford to travel very far to school. The travel expenses are too prohibitive. Flying back and forth for vacations can eat up almost as much money as tuition. Our research shows that the vast majority of our students come from within a hundred miles of campus."

Amy looked sadder and sadder the longer she listened. Maybe it was going to be harder to get to California than she had thought. Bill was now in high spirits, though. The meeting had turned out to be just as much of a circus as he had hoped it would be. When the officer closed by asking if there were any more questions, Bill grinned maliciously. "Amy?" he said, and made her blush.

The most detailed information about college I received at Bingham came from the school's library. Because the library had so few legitimate users, the head librarian, Miss Mead, tended to be on fairly intimate terms with the handful of regulars. She introduced herself on my second visit and we chatted frequently after that.

"Are you planning to go to college?" she asked one day.

"I think so," I said.

"Then you may be interested in some new equipment we just installed. It's a computer terminal with access to information about colleges and careers."

She gave me a library pass, and the next morning I signed out of my first-period study hall and went up to investigate. The computer equipment was in a converted storage room at one end of the library. There was a keyboard with a printout device, and another keyboard hooked up to an old black-and-white Magnavox TV. The computer equipment was a real boon to the school, because before it was purchased the data processing course had had to make do with a cardboard model of a terminal, something like a silent piano, which the students could practice on. The teacher would bring in printouts from real computers—things like grocery store inventories and long, coded lists of automobile parts—and the students would pretend they were calling them up from the big cardboard box.

The librarian sat me down at the terminal and asked me what kind of career I thought I wanted. "Well," I said, "I guess I've been thinking about being a reporter." She consulted a paperback catalog and then typed in some numbers. The machine spewed out a couple of feet of green-and-white perforated paper:

662 REPORTER
JOB DESCRIPTION:
Collects and analyzes information about newsworthy events to write news stories for publication or broadcast. Receives assignments or evaluates leads to develop story idea. Gathers and verifies information through interview, observation and research. Organizes material, determines emphasis and writes story according to prescribed editorial style and format standards. Requires good vocabulary, organizational skills, attention to details and ability to work with people. Indications are that through 1985 employment potential for this occupation will be good in CA, CT, DE, HI, IL, IA, KS, KY, ME, MA, NE, OR, PA, TX and UT.

"Now," Miss Mead said, "would you like the names of some schools where you could get a good education in journalism?"

"Sure."

"Which part of the country are you mainly interested in?"

I weighed this question and decided on New England, since I had actually gone to school there. Miss Mead typed in some more numbers. The machine whirred:

   12 Colleges qualify
194 Southern Connecticut State College 9
548 University of Maine-Orono 9
592 Boston University 9

600 Emerson College 9
625 North Adams State College 9
626 Northeastern University 9
638 Suffolk University 9
641 University of Massachusetts-Amherst 9
834 Keene State College 8
1294 Roger Williams College-Fulton 8
1298 University of Rhode Island 8
1465 St. Michael's College 9

Miss Mead left me alone at this point, and I looked into some other careers. Over the course of the next half hour, I found out what it takes to be a news writer, a technical news writer, a script writer, and a pastry chef, because I punched in the wrong numbers. Actually, pastry chef sounded interesting:

> Supervises and coordinates activities of cooks engaged in preparation of desserts, pastries, confections and ice cream. . . . Fashions table and pastry decorations. Orders supplies and equipment. Keeps production records. Requires organizational skills, background in pastry preparations and ability to direct workers.
> Indications are that through 1985, employment potential for this job will be good in most states, stable in DC, MT, NE, NY, RI and SD and limited in AK.

I wasn't sure whether AK was Alaska or Arkansas, so I decided to play it safe and avoid both.

There was another student in the computer room, Lou Minetta, Bingham's only National Merit Semifinalist. We weren't in any of the same classes—as school brain Lou took only the most advanced courses—but I had met him at lunch a couple of times and knew him well enough to talk to him. I asked him what he was doing.

"I'll show you," he said. He was sitting at the portable

keyboard, monitoring a vast and complicated array of numbers on the screen of the Magnavox. He sorted through a box of casette tapes, found the one he was looking for, and popped it into a portable tape recorder that was hooked up to the keyboard.

"This is a game that another kid and I invented. I wrote the program, we both typed it in. It took three periods just to do all the typing."

He opened his notebook and showed me the program. The thing was endless, page after page of numbers and symbols.

"How did you figure out how to do all that?" I asked.

"Oh, when they got the computer I just spent a couple of hours with the manual that came with it. It was all trial and error, but we finally figured it out. If I did this again, I could do it with a lot fewer instructions, but we were just playing it by ear when we started out."

"Did any of the teachers help you?" I asked.

Lou laughed. "I think I can safely say that at the moment I am the only person in this school who knows how to operate this machine. Which certainly makes it easy to get time on the terminal."

"Do you come here a lot?"

"All the time," he said. "I have study hall first period, and I come in every day. I'm the one who sets it up in the morning. They keep it locked up overnight. I've got study hall third period, too, so I come in then. The other guy has study hall second period, so between the two of us we probably account for ninety percent of its use. I even have to come in after school and take it apart so they can lock it up."

He typed in some numbers and the instructions of the game he had invented flashed onto the screen. The name of the game was "Attack"·

You are the commander of a pulse-powered intergalactic starship with Class A tactical and strategic capabilities. Your mission is to seek out and destroy an alien cruiser which has been conducting illegal offensive sorties in your district. However, because the alien ship is equipped with quasar-type wave-distortion mechanisms, your radar and other detection equipment are unable to pinpoint the craft's precise coordinates. All that your sensing devices are able to do is to provide you with your margin of error every time you fire a salvo.

I tried my hand at the controls but was quickly decimated by the alien ship.

"You're not paying attention to the error information," Lou said. "You sort of have to triangulate to figure out where the alien is." He took his turn and destroyed the alien craft on his third salvo.

"Lucky shot," I said.

Lou chuckled slyly. "And now," he said, "I will aim my phasers at you."

11
∾ "Them Little Numbers"

Back in the eighth grade, when I took my first algebra course, one of the guys in my class was baffled for most of the first week. He just couldn't figure out what x was supposed to be. He tried everything he could think of but he couldn't get it to work out the same two times in a row. Seemed like x had a different value in every equation he tried. Our math teacher could scarcely find words to explain what was the matter.

I was never quite so lost as my friend was, but even so I did not have an easy time in math. I couldn't seem to understand anything until after we had been tested on it. In eleventh grade, while most of my friends dug into their first year of calculus, I signed up for a gut course called "Pre-Calculus," which was really just a simplified rehash of the Algebra II I had taken the year before. The next year I took no math at all and felt warm all over when I realized I would never have to take it again.

I was quite surprised, therefore, when I found myself enjoying Advanced Math at Bingham. Suddenly algebra was making sense to me. At home I started taking my math book to the dinner table and doing my homework while I ate. It drove Ann crazy, but I felt as though a veil had been lifted from my eyes. My original plan had been to do no homework at all in any of my classes, except when I had an assignment that had to be handed in. I figured it would be easier to put in an "average" perform-ance if I didn't know the material and had to guess than if I did know it and had to decide what sort of responses would be appropriate for a high school student. In English and history I looked at my books only enough to determine what was being covered, and then relied on whatever I could remember from college and high school. Which wasn't usually very much. But in math I was completely carried away. My new feel for a discipline that had always eluded me gave me an enthusiasm I found difficult to control. I was even doing the extra-credit problems, although I didn't hand them in. And then, on our first test, I got the highest score in the class.

I felt guilty about doing so well, but even though my grade was the highest it wasn't terribly good, all things considered. I got 54 points out of a possible 60, which works out to 90 percent. Since the test was intended merely to see how much we remembered from Algebra II, which all of my classmates had taken the year before, I figured everybody would do well. But no one did. The next highest grade after mine was 40 points, or 66 percent, which at Bingham was just one point above passing (in math, as in most of my classes, our grades were often read aloud).

Oddly enough, my classmates' difficulties on the test were more verbal than mathematical. The quiz dealt solely with definitions of basic algebraic terms, and the concepts it covered were the sort that are disposed of in the introductory chapters of all algebra books. Anyone with even vague recollec-tions of Algebra II ought to have been able to figure out most of them, and this was a class of good students. Advanced Math was limited to kids who had earned grades of B or higher in Algebra II. They weren't the most advanced students in the school— those were the ones taking calculus—but they were near the top. Their main problem on the test was in expressing clearly what by now they knew more or less intuitively.

One of the questions on the test asked us to define a "product." I wrote, "X is a product if there are real numbers A and B so that $A \times B = X$," which is more or less right. I hadn't memorized that definition, but with a little thought I was able to figure out what it ought to include. I knew it would have to be specific enough to be binding and yet general enough to cover all the possibilities. It was an easy question and everyone should have been able to come close. But the vast majority of my classmates defined product simply as "answer." They had similar difficulties with almost all the questions. The first one was a fill-in-the-blank, "A set is a ——— of ——— objects." The proper answer is, "A set is a group of well-defined objects." I didn't quite have that, but I came close enough to receive credit. Most of my classmates, though, were way out in left field (even to the point of ignoring that the word "objects" had been supplied): A "A set is a set of various objects"; "a set is a pair of brackets"; "a set is a number of things"; "a set is a group of numbers"; "a set is a set of subsets."

People who worry about the continuing decline in SAT scores almost always treat the drops in the math and verbal parts as separate phenomena. But in my math class, mathematical difficulties were very often verbal in origin. Several students referred to mathematical variables (X and Y, for example) only as "letters." I heard one boy refer to exponents, the superscript numerals in expressions like "X^3 or $E = mc^2$," as "them little numbers." A student who can't find words to express basic mathematical principles is handicapped before he even tries to attack a problem.

Some of the class's difficulties could be traced directly to our textbook, which was written in such harrowing language that even our teacher had trouble deciphering it: "The sign of a signed numeral is the sign that precedes it or is understood to precede it"; "We shall deal with those nonlinear inequalities whose left members can be factored into linear factors and those that are fractions with the unknown in the denominator and probably also in the numerator." Textbook publishers compete so fiercely with one another for the limited (and shrinking) markets that they continually throw out good books in favor of new editions too hastily put together. The authors of our text had apparently felt so compelled to be different that they had abandoned a number of standard terms and replaced them with new ones that were supposedly more logical or meaningful. As a result, a lot of my classmates found themselves in the dark a good deal of the time. The very vocabulary of algebra had shifted beneath them.

Mr. Pottle, our teacher, made a valiant effort. "These books are actually college-level," he told us, "and they're more confusing than they have to be, but there's nothing we can do about that until they wear out." Mr. Pottle eventually abandoned the book, except as a source of homework problems, and gave us mimeographed handouts explaining the explanations in the chapters. "We used to have a great book in this course," he said, "but you can't buy it anymore. They took it off the market."

Mr. Pottle reminded me so much of one of my high school math teachers that twice I called him by the other man's name. He had the tough, no-nonsense approach that is the stock in trade of successful high school math teachers. Math could be conquered by sheer persistence—that was the impression he gave. You didn't have to be a genius, you just had to make the effort. He wrote everything out on the blackboard in huge, legible script and checked over our computations on homework assignments so meticulously there could never be any doubt where a problem had gone wrong. Most of the kids in the class thought he was too hard—Amy Kendris told me she could never understand any of his explanations—but almost everybody liked him. When he was sick for two weeks and we had a substitute fresh out of college, the complaints were immediate.

"That's not the way Mr. Pottle does that," Amy said.

"I'm not Mr. Pottle," the woman said.

"No, you're not."

Almost everyone stopped doing homework while the substitute was there (even I did). She kept trying to give metaphorical explanations of mathematical principles in the book—"Try to think of a function as a *vending machine*"—but no one was interested. When Mr. Pottle finally returned, he got a reception he couldn't have expected.

"That substitute lady thought she was Young Miss College Professor, man," Greg Liszk said.

Mr. Pottle was unflatterable. "You don't seem to have done a whole heck of a lot of work while I was out," he said. "There's a lot of material we're going to have to make up."

"She had all these *teaching methods*," Greg added.

In addition to his Advanced Math sections, Mr. Pottle taught a course in remedial math for kids who were having trouble with computation and basic concepts. "I had to spend five minutes this morning convincing them that eleven times eleven is a hundred and twenty-one and not a hundred and eleven," he told us one day. "The trouble with New Math, which is what you and everybody else in the country studies, is that it doesn't pay attention to the basic operations, like addition and multiplication. Back in the Stone Age when I was in school, you had to *know* what eleven times eleven was. You had to learn multiplication tables. Now they give you a handful of different-colored sticks and worry more about whether you know what base three is than whether you can add and subtract."

Mr. Pottle's remedial course was designed for the victims of New Math. "What a zoo that class is," he said. "I don't want you folks to get the impression that *you* don't give me headaches —believe me, you do—but compared with those guys, coming into this class is like dying and going to heaven."

"We're angels, right, Mr. Pottle?" one of the girls said.

"Or something," he said. "The hardest thing with the remedial group was just getting them motivated. The level they need the real help at is so elementary that they laughed when I gave them their first assignment. They said, 'Man, we don't need this stuff. It's easy.' Then they did the problems and I'd say on the average they got maybe ten percent of them right. So I went over to one of the big department stores and got a big stack of job applications from their clerical department. The forms had a little mathematical computation section, because you need some dexterity with figures to do that kind of work. Next day I handed out the forms in class and had the kids all fill them out. Then I gave them to my brother-in-law, who's the district representative of a large corporation, and asked him to read and critique them. I told him to say whatever he thought, to react as though he was actually reviewing applicants for a beginning position. The guy was *merciless*. Then I brought them all back and handed them out without comment, and from then on I didn't have any trouble."

A couple of the boys laughed.

"Laugh while yet ye may, ladies and gentlemen," Mr. Pottle said. "I've been thinking about making another trip over to that store."

Mr. Pottle never did bring us any job applications, but one day he came to class with a boxful of pamphlets.

"I don't know what kind of information you kids are getting about college," he said, "but a few of you, anyway, might be interested in this."

The pamphlets contained information about an SAT preparation program at a local university. For $150 you could take a twenty-seven-hour review course in math and English designed to improve scores on the SAT.

"A hundred and fifty bucks may sound like an awful lot of money," he said, "but I've seen it make a difference. The common wisdom is that coaching doesn't improve SAT scores, but I know kids who went up fifty and a hundred points. Advanced Math is good SAT preparation, but there's stuff that'll be on the tests that we won't even get to until the end of the year. I'm not really *advising* it, you understand, but you should know what the options are."

Mr. Pottle spent two or three entire periods during the semester just giving us information about college. For some of the kids in the class, I suspect, it was the only information they got. Mr. Pottle knew the limitations of the Guidance Department and he had decided to do something himself.

"I don't know how many of you have been going to these meetings they've been having with representatives of colleges," he said, "but you should all take advantage of them. No one will ever tell you this, but at a lot of those meetings, the representatives actually take notes on the kids who show up. If you eventually go to the school, those notes go right into your admissions folder. They'll tell you they don't do it, but believe me, they use every piece of information they can get their hands on. It might be that the fact that you made a good impression at one of those meetings was the thing that tipped the balance in your favor." He paused. "Of course, it could work the other way, too."

"Like with me," Greg Liszk said, smiling.

"I wasn't thinking of anyone in particular."

Greg laughed. "I guess I better not go to any of those meetings, huh?"

"Oh, you should go all right," Mr. Pottle said. "Just don't sign your name to anything."

Greg Liszk was the boy with all the beer who had sat next to me on the train ride to the Who concert the month before. He had a reputation for being a classroom cutup, but he was smart and Mr. Pottle enjoyed sparring with him in a friendly way every now and then. I got the impression that Mr. Pottle had been a cutup himself at some point in his past. Now he was all business, but he tolerated a good joke. He was about forty and had short, carefully combed black hair. He was the only teacher I had who wore a tie every day. He wanted us to know that he was the one in charge. And at the heart of his authority was a genuine concern for the futures of his students. Our classroom performance couldn't have made him very optimistic, and that was why he spent so much time encouraging us to think ahead.

One day he held up a mimeographed sheet that he had found in his mailbox that morning.

"I know you are probably tired of hearing me go on and on about college," he said, "but you may have noticed the 'open houses' that some of the colleges have been scheduling. This is an announcement about one of them." He passed the sheet around. "You should check it out. What happens is you go up to the campus and talk to some of the admissions people and then they have students available to show you around the school. You can sit in on classes and check out the dormitories and ask questions and that sort of thing."

"Free beer?" Greg asked.

"Now let me close my eyes," Mr. Pottle said, "and see if I can guess who asked that question."

"Just wondering."

"Anyway," Mr. Pottle said, "I used to give these tours when I was in school."

"Was that in the Mezozoic or the Paleozoic era?" someone asked.

"All right, settle down. We can always go back to factoring if you aren't interested." He looked at us sternly. "Anyway, if you're going to be living in a place for the better part of four years, you want a pretty good idea of what you're in for. No admissions officer is ever going to tell you that the dorm rooms are too small or that there's no place within fifty miles to go out and have a beer. Just go on up and pretend you're a student— nobody's gonna know the difference if you don't tell them—and see if it feels right."

12
Girls

What it means to be a teenager has changed since I was one, and the differences are most conspicuous among the girls. Girls are surer indicators of shifting teenage moods than boys are, because female society in a high school is more elaborate, and hence more visible, than male society. Proms, homecomings, dances with themes—the rituals one thinks of first when one thinks of high school—are essentially feminine celebrations. High school rings, like fraternity pins, exist to be given to girls.

Toward the end of the sixties, though, everything changed for the girls. At high schools all around the country, proms were canceled, homecoming coronations were parodied or abandoned, the traditional "date" shriveled up and, in its old form, practically disappeared. All this affected the boys, of course, but for them the new game was being played by familiar rules. Drugs instead of drinking, politics instead of hell-raising. Teenage political rebellion in the sixties was mostly a male experience, the male rites of passage blown out of proportion. Demonstrations were like pep rallies without the fussiness. The new radical organizations were blatantly sexist institutions. The boys were in control, the old structures were either gone or weakened, and the girls were left in the lurch.

Now the old order is reemerging, and the girls show the change most clearly. The boys in my class at Bingham seem more familiar to me in many ways than the girls do. Superficially, at least, they are the boys I knew ten years ago, minus some angst. The girls, on the other hand, seem brand new. They are a throwback to something older. When I described them to Julia over the phone she said, "My God, those are the people *I* went to high school with." She would recognize the boys, too, but with them the identification would take a little longer.

It was a dark, rainy day. Mrs. Medina, our accounting teacher, was absent, the substitute was a pushover, and no one was doing any work. Like virtually all of the boys in the class, I was tipping perilously backward in my chair and staring into space. A student council representative was peddling Snickers bars and M&Ms at fifty cents a shot. The girls were talking full volume:

"How much are the Snickers?"

"Don't buy it, Dawn."

"Why not?"

"Somebody has to say no."

Dawn made a move for the candy box. Sherry grabbed her hand.

"No! Don't do it!"

"But I'm hungry."

"You know you have a problem. You have to be careful."

"But *Sherry*."

"Dawn, stop it."

"But I'm *better*. Yesterday I didn't have hardly anything. I had a Snickers, and some cookies, and a piece of pie. And that's *all* I ate. All day long."

"That's just the problem. It's all junk food."

"Pie?"

"You should eat real food."

"This morning I had real food: toast."

"How many pieces?"

"Two."

"Then you can't have no more today."

"Sherry."

"You want to get all fat again like you used to be?"

"I wasn't *fat.*"

"Yes, you were."

"I was just a little chubby. I was a *big* girl."

"Oh, you was big all right."

"That's not nice."

A boy interrupted: "One fucking candy bar isn't going to hurt."

"She's been eating too much chocolate. Just look at her face."

"That's not from chocolate. That's from some Pond's I rubbed into my face."

"Why did you do that?"

"I wanted my cheeks to be *smooth.*"

"You ought to use Formula Nineteen. It's a cleanser for your face."

"My face used to be like yours, Sherry. I *never* had pimples. You remember."

"I never noticed your face. I was too busy looking at your fat."

"That's not *nice.*"

"You just use Formula Nineteen and you won't get no pimples. But when you use it, Dawn, you have to use a moisturizer."

"Don't use the moisturizer they give you. It's too greasy."

"Don't use no soap neither."

Dawn finally gave in and went without a Snickers. Sherry, meanwhile, had bought some M&Ms.

"Thank you, Sherry. If it wasn't for you, I would have bought that candy bar."

"You would have finished it by now."

"Thanks for making me not."

"That's okay. I don't mind. *Somebody*'s got to help you."

A good ten percent of the girls in my class were named Dawn, or Daun, or even Daune. And most of them looked pretty much the same. High school girls maintain order and stability within the species by agreeing on a single, unflattering style and then sticking with it at all costs. The fashion consensus at Bingham when I was there was reflected primarily in the shoes. Almost without exception, the girls wore cumbersome wooden clogs or ungainly earth-type shoes with thick rubber soles, all of which looked like prosthetic devices. For variety, grim little laminated high heels called "slides" were tolerated. The hairstyles were mostly Neo-Revisionist Farrah Fawcett, blown dry and held together with static, spit, and Final Net. Girls who deviated from the norm usually spent the whole day wishing they hadn't: "Ohhh! Gayle! I love your shoes! They're so . . . *thin!*"

One day Sherry of the Snickers episode came to school with her hair a new color. Actually it was several colors: white, red, and a little brown. The night before a friend of hers had tried to frost it with some new, inexpensive preparation they had seen advertised on TV. Now Sherry and her friend were not speaking.

"It doesn't look bad at *all,*" Dawn said when Sherry came into accounting.

"You shoulda seen it before," Sherry said. "It was all white and everything, except at the ends. I just sat in my room and cried. Then my mom took me over to the hairdresser and they neutralized it."

"It doesn't look so bad," Dawn said.

"What color were you trying to make it?" another girl asked.

"I was trying to frost it, but the stuff all leaked under the cap. I'm gonna kill that girl."

"Don't worry," Dawn said. "It'll all grow out."

A boy walked into the class and stopped dead in his tracks. "For Christ's sake, girl," he said, "what the fuck did you do to your hair?"

"Ohhh," Sherry moaned. "It *does* look bad."

"Bad ain't the word for it," the boy said as he sat down.

"You just don't pay any attention," Dawn said. "It's all going to work out just fine."

Other than fat, hair, and looks in general, the girls' prime topic of conversation was boys. And a surprising proportion of the boy talk was conducted, like the Snickers debate, at full volume in classrooms crowded with boys. For the most part, the boys sat oblivious while the female voices swelled around them. We just tilted silently in our chairs and pretended not to pay attention. Or maybe the other guys really *weren't* paying attention. But I sat quietly and took notes on the sly.

"Is that an engagement ring?" Lisa asked Susan one day when Mrs. Medina was absent again (she had an unnamed "condition" that kept her out of school a lot).

Susan held out her hand. "This? Are you kidding? If I got this as an engagement ring I'd throw it in the guy's face."

"When I get engaged, I want at least one carat."

"When *I* get engaged, my hand is going to *drag on the ground.*"

"I want heart-shaped, emerald-cut, or traditional."

"I don't care about shape, I care about size. I want *big.* It's going to be mounted in white gold and have about twenty little diamonds all around it. But not *too* little. I want one of them star saphires that are blue and have a white star in the middle. My aunt had one of them and, brother, it cost a fortune."

"When are you getting engaged?" the substitute teacher asked Susan.

"What—me?" She laughed. "Maybe in about ten years."

"Hey, Susan," another girl called, "you still go with Tom Borowski?"

"Yeah. How did you know? I've been going with him for eight months."

"He lives near Eisenhower, right?"

"Yeah."

"I know his brother Bill."

"I ain't never met him."

"I never met Tom. Isn't he in college?"

"Yeah, but he's quitting next month. He says he don't like it, the stupid jerk."

"Are you going to the Winter Cotillion with him?" (The cotillion was still close to two months away.)

"Yeah, the stupid jerk. But I told him he's gotta rent a black or a white tuxedo, and wear a white or a pink ruffled shirt, and give me yellow roses, and take me to a seafood dinner that costs at least fifteen bucks, or I ain't going."

Popular girls, like successful armies, depend on impeccable lines of communication. A good deal of every high school girl's day is spent in close communication with other high school girls. They confer at lunch, hold meetings in the halls, write long letters to each other in class. The idea isn't necessarily to exchange information: A lot of the communication that goes on is intended merely to facilitate other communication. Girls begin to worry if their friends are not in constant touch with them.

When actual conversation isn't possible, girls write letters. More secret notes changed hands every day in the halls of Bingham High School than at an international summit conference. A few of these notes came into my possession. One of them I found wadded up in a desk, one I found on the floor, one I copied over the shoulder of the girl who was writing it, and one I was shown by a boy who had intercepted it.

Dear Cary,

I decided to write you a note because I can't read even tho I have to. I have to finish this book and do a report by Fri. I was talking to Al today and I think I understand him. He doesn't really know what is going on. I think you should try to let him understand what you might be feeling. He just wants to be good to you but I think that he doesn't know how. He tries to hard and so you think that he is being pushy but he doesn't think that he is. I think well I know he really likes you. He said he couldn't stop thinking all day about what you told him and didn't want to break up. I don't want to tell you what to do tho.

What do you want to do this weekend? I want to go to a movie alright. Do you have to work tonight? I can't wait to hear from GEORGE. Have you talked to Daun today? She is UNEXPLAINABLE. Write me when you get this.

Sally

Melissa,

yes you do care about her right! and it will happen again cause I know.

Lu

Joe,

hi. i was sitting here thinking of writing a letter to my brother but thought of you. we said we were going to write to each other often? I guess it seems like we have both forgotten totally. i know its probly my fault because you have less time than I do. If you don't want to all you have to do is write and tell me so.

i'm sorry about my handwriting but its never been any good at all. How come you never wrote back after my last letter to you. I thought you meant it as a hint to stop writing to you but I decided to write again. And when (if) you do write back fill me in on your year and are there any new or old "loves" in your life? You'll always be one in mine.

i really missed you after you left and I grew tired of watching tv and all. I played alot of tennis the last week and did a lot of hiking. I was totally bored. it's too bad it took us so long to "finally" meet each other. But I'm glad we did. The night you came over to watch tv and were so jumpy about when the parents were coming home, they didn't come back til 2:13. I was watching the worst movie.

I shouldn't be boring you with all this but theres no one awake now (3:05 am) to talk to. I love ya.

Well I guess I better get some sleep.

All my love,
Lisa

WRITE BACK
ps. What grade are you in? When's your birthday? and can you please send a picture of yourself? I'll try to write interestinger next time.

dear Frank:
just to let you know I'm thinking about you every minute. I cant wait until this weekend.

I totally love ya,
You know who

13
∾ Dancing

The sign in the cafeteria took up most of the back wall:

THE BINGHAM HIGH SCHOOL STUDENT COUNCIL PRESENTS
A FIFTIES SOCK HOP
ROCK AROUND THE CLOCK WITH BIG VIC AND THE VICEROYS
8:00 pm to 11:00 pm
Saturday October 13, 1979
$3.00 per person

The sign was spelled out in big purple construction-paper letters. In the center of the display was a huge paper alarm clock with hands and feet and a smiling face. By lunchtime, a drooling tongue had been added to the face and the words had been changed to read, A FIFTIES COCK HOP, LICK AROUND THE DICK. Two representatives of the student council had to find a ladder in the storeroom and move everything a few feet closer to the ceiling while the principal looked on, scowling. The first lunch shift came streaming in just as the revision got under way, and a loud chorus of boos went up. The principal went to the public address system to restore order.

In math Amy Kendris asked me if I was going to the sock hop.

"I guess so," I said.

"I am, too."

"Is Bill going?"

"I doubt it. Are you going to take somebody?"

"Yeah," I said. This was sheer conjecture. I hadn't gotten around to asking Ann yet.

"Who?" Amy asked.

"Her name is Ann. She doesn't go here."

"My boyfriend doesn't go here either."

"Is that who you're going with?"

"Yeah, probably. He hates to dance, though. Do you have your tickets yet?"

"No."

"Me either."

I bought my tickets after school that day and showed them to Ann when I got home.

"There's a dance at school next week," I said.

"And?"

"And, well, I was wondering if you wanted to go. You know, like a date."

"Hmmmm."

"It's a fifties sock hop, but you don't have to get all dressed up for it. We can just go as we are, and we don't have to stay very long if you don't want to."

She finally agreed. I figured she would have a good time. We would go out to dinner beforehand and drop in on the dance just long enough to see what was going on. If it seemed like fun we could spend the night in Bingham and come back the next day.

A few days later, Bill Scalet and I were talking at lunch.

"So," he said, "I hear you're going to the dance."

"Yeah. Where'd you hear that?"

"Amy told me."

"Are you going?"

"Me? Shit no."

"How come?"

"Oh, I don't know, man. I don't have a car, for one thing."

"I don't either."

"It's too much of a drag to go to one of these things if you don't have a car. Either your parents or somebody else's have to take you. You going with somebody?"

"Yeah."

"Who?"

"You don't know her. She doesn't go here."

"Eisenhower?"

"No." I wasn't sure what to say. I hadn't made up a story for Ann yet. Well, you see, I have this *wife*. "She goes to college," I said.

"No shit? How old?"

"Twenty."

"Christ, man, a fossil. You like older women, eh?"

"I met her over the summer. In New York. My aunt was a friend of her parents."

"Good-looking?"

"Yeah," I said, "considering her age."

The dance was a disaster from start to finish. We arrived in Bingham two hours before it started and went to the center of town to look for a restaurant. It was a Saturday night, so I thought we'd have several places to choose from, but everything was closed. We walked for blocks. Nothing. Finally we went into a tiny all-night grocery store and bought some potato chips and Cokes. Ann was not pleased.

"Hey," I said. "Teenagers live on this stuff."

"I am not a teenager."

"I know. You're twenty."

"Twenty?"

"Yeah. I told my friends you were twenty."

"Didn't think I could pass for seventeen?"

"It's not that. You look younger than I do. I just want to be covered in case you don't *act* like you're seventeen."

We had lots of time to kill, so we went on a tour of the neighborhood. About half a mile up the road we passed a drive-in restaurant I had forgotten about completely. But the place was crawling with teenagers, so we decided not to go in. Besides, we were full of potato chips.

We walked for about an hour. I had thought wives were supposed to be interested in seeing where their husbands worked, but I guess Ann saw more of Bingham than she wanted. She also saw a lot of my schoolmates. There were dozens of them out on the streets, and they were all wearing fifties-style clothes.

"I thought you said we didn't have to get dressed up for this," Ann said.

"We don't. Everybody won't be dressed up. And anyway, you wouldn't be any happier right now if you were wearing saddle shoes, would you?"

"I don't want to go."

"It's too late."

"No it's not."

"Don't worry. Everything will be fine. Just think of it as an adventure."

A little after eight o'clock, we headed over toward the school. The dance was in the gymnasium and we had to go around to the back to get in. On the way we passed a group of fifteen or twenty kids who were getting high and smashing an occasional beer bottle on the street.

"Even *they* are dressed up," Ann said. The boys were wearing leather jackets.

"They don't count," I said. "Those guys dress like that all the time."

We went inside. The principal was at the door, checking tickets He had dressed up, but peculiarly: He was wearing high-water overalls, a torn T-shirt, clodhoppers, and a straw hat. Maybe he thought it was a square dance. He examined our tickets closely, then directed us over to a long table at which half of the student council was seated. All tickets were numbered, and the student council members had long master lists of names and numbers. If your name did not appear on the list, or if you had a ticket other than the one you had been sold, you couldn't go inside. No tickets were available at the door. We passed inspection and went into the gym.

Unfortunately for me, virtually everyone in the place had dressed up. The girls were all wearing billowy "poodle" skirts and enormous white shirts borrowed from their fathers, and the boys had slicked back their hair with Brylcreme or Vaseline or Crisco. Ann looked over the crowd and passed judgment: "All the girls in your class are fat."

We crossed over to the other side of the gym to sit in the bleachers along the wall. We almost didn't get there. The floor had been covered with dance wax, which Ann had never run into before, and she nearly fell down

"I hate this," she said.

Out on the floor, two or three hundred of my classmates were bunny-hopping in a long, winding chain that encircled two dozen couples jitterbugging down near the bandstand. Big Vic and the Viceroys were playing "Blue Suede Shoes." I realized how few boys there were in the gym; they were outnumbered ten to one by girls. And there was only one boy bunny-hopping: He had wispy hair and a big nose and his pants were too short and too baggy. Ann and I had seen him come in with his date, a quiet girl in my accounting class.

I put my arm around Ann's shoulder and banged my elbow against the bleachers. She stared straight ahead. Amy Kendris looked over as she bounced by in the bunny line. "Try and look like you're having a good time," I hissed at Ann. "I have to see these people every day." She sat up stiff as a board.

A cheerleader I knew from journalism was standing about twenty feet away from us. She didn't seem to be with a boy; she was talking to another girl and practicing the splits. Half a dozen football players in letter jackets came in and shuffled across the floor looking bored and awkward. They stood on the sidelines for a few minutes, then left. Dawn Lavin came in with her boyfriend, who was on crutches. She helped him climb into the bleachers one section down from us. They sat way up on the top row and surveyed the scene. The boy kept pointing things out with his crutch. Both he and Dawn were wearing ordinary clothes.

"What do you expect?" Ann said. "Her date is a cripple."

Two kids I didn't recognize were sprawled in the bleachers about twenty feet away from us. They were necking furiously. After ten minutes or so, the girl went off with a girl friend to dance, leaving the boy looking proud and satisfied in his seat. He leaned way back into the bleachers, stretched out his arms, and smiled. His conquest, meanwhile, was hugging her friend and telling all.

"Can't you try to look like you're having a good time?" I said to Ann. "You look really bored."

"I am really bored."

"We could dance."

"No."

"Let me put my arm around you at least."

"No."

So there we sat, looking very much like a couple of seventeen-year-olds having a very bad time at a dance. I was frantic. I didn't want my friends to think I was striking out, but every time I made a move I looked like a fool. Blessedly, few of my friends were actually there. I saw Jim Devaney strolling around dejectedly with an unlit cigarette in his mouth, and I spotted half a dozen people I knew from my classes, but no one paid much attention to us.

Ann had a lot of good reasons for being upset. I had thrown her into this thing without much preparation. She had expected the dance to be small, and she had thought she would have a chance to talk to some of my friends; the idea of pretending she was someone else appealed to her. But the dance was big and noisy, and everyone was a stranger to her. High school dances just weren't her idea of a good time. She had only been to one, other than her senior prom, and she didn't have fond memories of it. Sitting in the bleachers with me was insult added to injury several times over. We hadn't even been able to eat dinner.

I, meanwhile, was alarmed to discover that whatever veneer of social ease I had managed to acquire since my own adolescence was perilously thin. I kept mumbling and banging my elbow into the bleachers and bumping the back of Ann's head with my hand. I was also sweating like a maniac. For an hour we were both in hell.

I was a little surprised at my reaction. I had been to lots of dances in junior high and high school, and had even presided over one as a student council president. I had, in fact, performed at a fifties sock hop: In eleventh grade I stood on the edge of a stage and sang "Hot Rod Lincoln" while my girl friend sat at my feet. Come to think of it, though, that one hadn't turned out very well either. I forgot the words halfway through the song and had to start again at the beginning while the band growled behind me. And almost immediately afterward my girl friend and I broke up for the sixtieth or seventieth time.

The band played "Love Me Tender" and the entire crowd on the dance floor, with the exception of about three couples, headed for the bleachers. No slow dancing for this group, apparently. I made one last try.

"Do you want to dance?"

"You can write anything about me you want," Ann said. "But I want to go home."

And so we left. A couple of kids were chatting in the doorway, still wearing their coats. Ann took a final skid on the dance wax, and we scooted past.

"Didn't you have any fun at all?" I asked her as we walked along.

"No."

"None?"

"None."

"Oh, well," I said, "thanks at least for coming. I guess I won't make you go to the Winter Cotillion with me."

She stopped. "You won't *make* me go?"

"I didn't mean it the way you think. I just meant, well, you don't have to go if you don't want to. I mean, I won't even *ask* you to go."

I don't think we exchanged more than two or three sentences all the way home.

In English the following Monday, the dance postmortem wasn't much rosier than the one that had taken place in our apartment over the weekend. Two girls and a boy were talking before class started.

"Did you go to the dance?"

"Yes," the boy said.

"I didn't see you there."

"I saw *you* there."

"I saw him there. He was sitting in the bleachers the whole time."

"No, I wasn't."

"He *was* sitting down part of the time."

"Maybe he was only resting."

"I sat down *very* rarely."

"And usually alone."

"*You* were the one who was in the bleachers the whole time."

"You didn't even see me."

"Yes, I did."

"Oh, yeah? What was I wearing?"

"Sweater and a black skirt with gold horizontal stripes."

"Well, *you* certainly have a good memory."

"What were you doing, staring at her?"

"Hah!"

"What's so 'hah' about that?"

"If I was staring at you it was only because I couldn't believe how totally retarded you looked."

"Owww, owww, help! I'm a retard! I'm mortally wounded! I'm bleeding to death!"

"Somebody get that girl an ambulance."

14

"A Boat of Nowhere"

We were reading aloud from tattered paperback copies of E. Talbot Donaldson's prose translation of *Beowulf*. The Geatish hero and his band of warriors had just arrived on the shores of Denmark. They had sailed from Geatland to do battle with Grendel, the insatiable demon who had been depopulating Denmark for twelve long years. On the beach when Beowulf and his men arrived was a Danish soldier charged with watching his native shores. "Why," Mr. Quennell, our English teacher, asked, "was there a guard on the coast of Denmark?" What he wanted us to say was that the Danes, dangerously weakened by the rampaging monster, were especially vulnerable to surprise attack by human enemies and had therefore posted a sentry. Mr. Quennell repeated his question: "Why was there a guard?" One by one my classmates began to raise their hands.

"To look after the boat?"

"No."

"To take them to the king?"

"No."

"To bring them food?"

"Now wait a second. Think before you answer."

"To guard against Grendel?"

"No, it was not to guard against Grendel. Grendel was already in their country. It would not have done any good to guard against him on the beach."

"To keep Grendel from leaving?"

"I'll give you a hint. The chances are there wasn't a guard there thirteen years ago. Why is that?"

"What did he say?"

"He said, Why wasn't there a guard there thirteen years ago?"

"Because the leaders of Denmark have learned the lesson of *Beowulf*?"

"What? What are you talking about?"

"Because in 1968 they didn't need an army anymore."

"It was because they had jet fighters."

"What on earth are you talking about?"

"He doesn't mean thirteen years *ago,* he means thirteen years *before.*"

"So *now* you tell me."

"Before what?"

"What?"

"Thirteen years before what?"

"Before when they're writing about, duh."

"Before Beowulf arrived."

"Anyway, 1968 is only eleven years ago, not thirteen."

"Have you all gone insane?"

"To protect against the Danes?"

"These *are* the Danes."

"No, they're not. They're the Geats."

"Same diff."

"Are they the Danes or the Geats?"

"Never mind about that. Just answer the question."

"To guard the coast."

"Why?"

"To protect the country?"

"Why did the country need to be protected?"

"Because of Grendel?"

"Why because of Grendel?"

"Because the country was so weak?"

"Why was it weak?"

"Because Grendel was eating up all the men."

"Yes."

"Then it *was* to keep out Grendel."

"No!"

"Will someone please tell me what page we're on?"

"Because Grendel was eating all the soldiers."

"And . . . ?"

"So it was safer on the beach?"

"No. No, no, no, no, no."

"Tell us!"

"Think!"

"There was a lone guard on the beach because everyone else was dead."

"No."

"Give us a hint."

"I gave you a hint."

"Give us another."

"All right, all right. If the country was very weak, which it was, what would happen if invaders came from across the sea and attacked it?"

"They would win."

"So?"

"So they put a guard on the beach."

"Why?"

"To tell them if anyone was coming."

"At last. The country was easier for an enemy to beat. They needed a guard to tell them if an enemy was coming so there couldn't be a surprise attack. They needed to be extra careful. Enough!"

After a moment of silence, Bill Scalet raised his hand. "What I want to know is, if Grendel came to the mead hall every night for twelve years and ate up all the men, why did the men keep going back to the mead hall?"

Mr. Quennell earned his bachelor's degree at a tiny teachers college in a rural section of the state. He majored in English, he told us one day, because he knew he wasn't any good at any of the other subjects. "It wasn't until later," he said, "that I found out I wasn't any good at English, either." This, of course, was a joke. At college Mr. Quennell maintained a solid C-plus average in his literature courses. He also found time to run the college's film society, which he founded his freshman year. The film society screened vintage movies in the college auditorium on Friday and Saturday nights, and it was so successful that Mr. Quennell was nearly able to pay his way through school on his share of the proceeds. "The only trouble with getting so involved with extracurricular activities," he said, "was that it didn't leave you a whole lot of time for your schoolwork. I'd go to a football game or have a movie or something, and suddenly the week would be shot and I'd be a hundred pages behind in my reading and no way to get caught up."

We learned about the film society and other fragments from Mr. Quennell's past one day during class in the middle of September. We had covered all the assigned material by the middle of the period, and no one felt like starting anything new, so we spent the remaining twenty minutes just shooting the breeze. When one of the girls asked Mr. Quennell what courses he had taken in college, he began to unburden. Such conviviality was rare with him. He almost never mentioned his wife or his children or referred to any part of his life beyond the classroom. Most days he was in a sour mood. He had the haggard, preoccupied look of a man whose family is being held by kidnappers. He gave the impression that teaching English for him was not only boring but even painful. Each day before the class came to order he would sit brooding at his desk with his grade book open before him, quietly deducting points from the averages of those of us who continued to talk after the bell rang. His voice almost never varied in pitch or quickened with emotion, and when he read he tended to stumble over polysyllables.

Mr. Quennell was about forty-five and had an unevenly receding hairline and terrible teeth. What remained of his hair was a frosty brown. He had bushy triangular sideburns a shade redder than the hair on his head, and when he took off his glasses you half expected the sideburns to come off, too. He had three suits, which he wore in loose rotation: a brown one, a green one, and a dusky gold one. His shirts and vests were all of similar colors, and his overall visual effect was distinctly autumnal: He looked like an aerial view of Kansas on a dark November day.

Mr. Quennell lectured from a hardbound notebook for which his wife had devised a brightly colored paste-craft cover. The book contained transcriptions of relevant notes that Mr. Quennell had taken in college, along with excerpts from various critical works and a chronology of important events in English history. When we began to study a new literary work, or progressed from one major period to another, he would open the notebook to the appropriate page, prop his head up with his arm, and begin to read. By listening to the words he used you could tell when he was reading something that he himself had written, and when he was reading something that he had copied from a book. You could also tell when he was digressing from his notebook altogether in order to provide a bit of local color or shore up his argument with examples. When we began our study of the English medieval period, he said:

"The common man in the Middle Ages could see that the knight in all his glorious armor was not actually doing very much in a battle. The knights had fine horses and weapons but most of the battles were won by foot soldiers with their—what, long arrows? I don't know. Whatever they had. Spears. The knights weren't good for much in a battle because they were all loaded down with their armor and probably could barely even see what was going on through those visors. They were also primarily interested in, you know, impressing the ladies. The common man saw that the Church needed reforming, too. His faith in knights and the Church were decreasing, and his faith in himself was increasing. He got a lot of self-esteem in the Middle Ages. He said, 'Hey, I'm not a dirt farmer. I'm *doing* something. I'm winning all these wars by myself, and I don't even have any armor. And the Church is corrupt, too.' This led to humanism. Also, there was a poll tax. Does anybody know what a poll tax is? They used to have them down in the South. Probably still do."

A boy in the back of the room raised his hand: "A poll tax is a tax you have to pay in order to vote."

"Well, no," Mr. Quennell said after a long, uncertain silence. "It was a tax on your head, a head tax. You would have to pay a certain amount for everything in your house that had a head. Say, a cat would cost you five dollars, and a parakeet would cost you a couple of bucks, and your mother would be twenty bucks, and maybe your father would be fifty or a hundred. Even a week-old baby would be charged, no matter if it never earned a dollar in its life. They still have this down in Alabama or someplace. The peasants objected to it because they had the most children and so they had to pay the most tax."

The boy in the back row raised his hand again, but Mr. Quennell kept talking.

"Anyway," he said, "there was this poll tax, et cetera, and during this period the government becomes highly centralized under the feudal system. It was very much a pyramid kind of thing, with the serfs at the bottom and then the lords and the king at the top and so on. There were two things that kept people going in the medieval period: Christianity and feudalism. There was also chivalry. You had chivalry beginning with the Anglo-Saxons, who were fierce warriors with a deep and nearly spiritual devotion to courage and physical excellence, but they also had a gentle side, too. Now this gentle side becomes the in thing in medieval behavior."

The section of World Literature that I was in was an honors class, which meant that the literature we learned was more high-powered than the meager stuff doled out to the rank and file. It also meant that the registrar would automatically add five points to the grade averages on our transcripts to reflect the supposedly more demanding work we had put in as honors students. With this bonus, diligent students could push their averages into the stratosphere. The valedictorian at Bingham usually has a cumulative average of something like 99.8.

There were two other honors sections in senior English. One was more advanced than ours, the other less. The one above us was the Advanced Placement class, which was strictly for kids who were college-bound. Later in the year the A.P. students would be given a standardized test which, if their scores were high enough, would entitle them to receive college credit for the work they had done in high school. The A.P. students began their survey of World Literature with the *Odyssey* instead of *Beowulf*, where we had begun, and they had to write short papers on assigned topics every couple of weeks. They also had longer reading assignments than we did, sometimes twenty or even thirty pages a night.

In Mr. Quennell's class the longest overnight reading assignment we had all semester was ten consecutive pages of *Beowulf*, and we had to write only one paper, which wasn't due until January. Mr. Quennell was not himself an avid reader, and as a consequence he tended to go easy on the homework. Four or five pages was a typical assignment. Usually only two or three assignments were given in a week. It took us a full six weeks to plow through the fifty-five pages of our *Beowulf* translation; by the time we reached the end, some of the kids couldn't remember how the story had begun.

Virtually every time Mr. Quennell mentioned a writer, he managed to work in at least one hopeless reference to the length of his works. When we were reading about the Anglo-Saxons, he said, "If you are interested in King Arthur you might go over to the library and see if they have a copy of *Morte d'Arthur* by Malory. You'd never read it, though, unless you locked yourself in a room for the next three years without food or water or a telephone. I mean, that is a *long* book. But maybe you could find a shorter version."

Mr. Quennell's students were not, on the whole, any more excited about reading than he was. Bill Scalet told me he hadn't read a book that wasn't assigned in class since at least ninth grade. And he was the editor of the paper. In my first two months at Bingham I saw exactly four students (all of them girls, two of them black) carrying books that hadn't been assigned. The books were *The Bastard, The Exorcist, The Omen,* and *The Entity,* I thought I'd found another one day, but *Sarah T.: Portrait of a Teenage Alcoholic* turned out to be an assignment.

Mr. Quennell had a metal paperback-book rack in his classroom—the kind you see in drugstores and supermarkets—but there were no books in it. In fact, there were no books anywhere in the room, except for the piles of undistributed textbooks on the counter in the back and a few teacher's editions on Mr. Quennell's desk. There wasn't even a dictionary, although one would have come in handy from time to time. One day before class, the girl who was reading *The Omen* asked, "What's a jackal?" and Mr. Quennell said, "It's a demon, you know, a kind of gargoyle. It stands for evil." He asked why she wanted to know. She said it was in the book she was reading, which she held up so he could see the cover. "Oh, yes," Mr. Quennell said. "That was excellent. I hope they make another sequel."

If books got short shrift in Mr. Quennell's English class, they didn't do much better in the library. The Bingham High School library is a long rectangular room on the second floor of the building. It contains about 7,000 volumes (Miss Mead, the head librarian, told me she had 10,000 volumes, but I made my own estimate a few days later and decided she was fudging). Idle browsing, at least during the school day, is not encouraged. Bingham students are not allowed inside the library unless they have a pass from an instructor certifying that they have an actual need to be among books. When a boy in English asked Mr. Quennell for a pass early in the year, he turned him down. "What do you need to be in the library for?" Mr. Quennell asked. "I haven't assigned you any papers." Students who regularly visited the library during study halls risked being pegged as troublemakers.

Use of the library was unrestricted during the twenty minutes before school and the hour and thirty minutes after, but in the half dozen times I went to the library after school, I never saw another student, except two girls in the Ushers' Guild who worked as assistant librarians. One day Miss Mead asked me either to check out a book or to leave; I was a little angry at the time, but I could hardly blame her for wanting to close up early.

Before school, the library was a popular gathering spot. One couple met there every morning to whisper secrets and hold hands on top of one of the tables. Another regular came in to read the sports page. Other students peered in as they circuited the halls, to see if any of their friends were inside.

Even with all this traffic, I don't remember ever seeing anyone (except me) check out a book. One day I decided to make a systematic investigation. I picked a shelf at random in the fiction section and looked at the DATE DUE card in the back of every book on it. Not one of them had been checked out more

recently than 1973. Half the books had never been checked out
at all. I tried another shelf. This time one book (*Jaws*) had been
checked out as recently as 1977. I began pulling books from
other shelves. I was determined to find one book that had been
checked out during the present school year, which was then just
short of two months old. I finally found one (it took half an hour):
a large-type edition of *A Farewell to Arms,* which had been
taken out, and renewed, in October. Why a high school library
thought it necessary to stock a large-type edition I don't know.
But I do know that October 1979 was the first time this
particular one had been checked out since March 1974.

Actually, when I took a closer look at some of the titles on the
shelves, the apathy of the students was less mysterious. Book-
buying at Bingham apparently ground pretty much to a halt in
the 1960s, and most of the volumes had been purchased well
before that. The most standard of the old standards were well
represented, but there was little to spark the imagination of a
young person looking for some weekend entertainment. Here's
an unrandom sampling of titles from the fiction section:

*A Program for Christine; A Palatte for Ingrid; A Sundae for
Dot; Waiting for Willa; Rosemary Wins Her Cape; The Paris Hat;
The Magnificent Barb; Maggie of Barnaby Bay; The Voice of
Bugle Ann; The Daughter of Bugle Ann; Mary in Command;
Cathy and her Castle; Betsy and the Great World; Betsy Was a
Junior; Betsy and Joe.*

*Hospital Zone; Baffling Affair in the County Hospital; Nurse's
Dilemma in the Private Corridor; Sharon's Nursing Diary; Staff
Nurse; Special Nurse; Sue Barton, Student Nurse; Sue Barton,
Visiting Nurse; Sue Barton, Rural Nurse; Sue Barton, Senior
Nurse; Sue Barton, Superintendent of Nurses; Sue Morris, Sky
Nurse; Jane Arden, Registered Nurse; Hilda Baker, School
Nurse; Arlene Perry, Orthopedics Nurse; Penny Marsh, Supervi-
sor of Public Health Nurses.*

*Introducing Patti Lewis, Home Economist; Overseas Teacher;
Foreign Service Girl; Allison Day, Weather Girl; Marjorie Thur-*

man, *Lab Technician*; *Lois Thornton, Librarian*; *Jane Cameron,
School Marm*; *Vida Prescott, Attorney*; *Nora Meade, M.D.*; *The
Vet Is a Girl!*

The Muddy Road to Glory; *A Hatful of Glory*; *Guns in the
Heather*; *Swords in the North*; *Wings for Peace*; *Wings for Pete*;
Wings for Tomorrow; *Wait for Private Black*; *Storm the Last
Rampart*; *The Boy of the Lost Crusade*; *Phantom of the Blockade*;
The Dark Frigate; *Dim Thunder*; *Listen, the Drum!*; *Drums*; *The
Plums Hang High*; *Lost Island*; *Bright Island*; *Mystery Island*;
Jonica's Island; *On Land and Sea with Caesar.*

On Guard!; *Batter Up!*; *Jets Away!*; *Time of Trial*; *Time Trial*;
Trial by Ice; *Pro Hockey Comeback*; *Gridiron Challenge*; *Speed-
way Challenge*; *Hot Rod Rodeo*; *Star Kicker*; *Puck Garber*; *Man
in a Cage*; *Boy on Defense*; *Backstop Ace*; *Basketball Clown*;
Sideline Quarterback; *Stock Car Racer*; *The Vanishing Steamer*;
Sabre Pilot; *Crash Landing.*

It's Jolly!; *Buffalo and Beaver*; *Fight Like a Falcon*; *Ice Falcon*;
The Earl's Falconer; *The Eagle of the Ninth*; *Open Season*;
Horsecatcher; *Justin Morgan Had a Horse*; *The Crystal Horse*;
The Horse That Won the Civil War.

Every Monday in Mr. Quennell's class we were assigned
a new unit in our vocabulary book. Each unit consisted of
twenty vocabulary words, followed by four sections of fill-in-the-
blank exercises. The exercises were due on Wednesday. If we ran
out of things to do on Tuesday we were given the remainder of
the period to start on our exercises. On Friday we had a quiz.
When Mr. Quennell gave us our assignment on Monday, he
would read the list of new words in order to acquaint us with
them. In his breathless monotone, the words, definitions, and
examples all blurred together: "Heedless not paying attention
we were heedless of the danger laud honor with praise the
judges lauded the victorious athlete."

On our Friday quizzes, Mr. Quennell would read the words in the same voice and the same order and wait while we spelled and defined each one. Later he would choose ten for us to use in sentences on the backs of our papers. The words were not difficult, and most of my classmates did well on the tests, although there were many lapses. In an oral review one day, Bill defined precedent as "to save for later." Another boy defined infinitesimal as "sweet-sounding." Another defined inter as "to go away." Mr. Quennell was not always helpful. He did not, for instance, correct Bill when he misdefined precedent. And on one vocabulary exercise, in which we were asked to transform words from our list into other parts of speech, he took away points from anyone who did not give "revelation" as the noun form of the verb "to revel."

When my classmates complained, as they frequently did, about the books we were asked to read, their complaints usually had to do with either the obscurity of the vocabulary or the density of the text. *Beowulf* caused enormous difficulties. "What's the matter?" asked Patti Morgan, a girl who later switched classes. "Didn't they know how to write back in the Old Ages?" Several days later, as Mr. Quennell began his lecture, Patti sighed, "Here we go again, on a boat of nowhere."

Occasionally I was the one who had the difficulties. Our midterm vocabulary test included an "Analogy" section in which we were given incomplete verbal analogies and asked to complete them with appropriate words from a master list: "renegade is to temerity as defamation is to ———"; "retribution is to precedent as blame is to ———"; "phlegmatic is to chagrin as revel is to ———." I puzzled over this section for many minutes and made several errors in filling it out. I expected my classmates to be up in arms about the inanity of the questions, but it turned out that few of them had found the analogies troublesome. Somehow they and Mr. Quennell had been tuned to the same wavelength.

When Mr. Quennell tested us on our reading, the quizzes

invariably consisted of fifteen or twenty factual questions about whatever work we were studying at the time. *When did Grendel attack? What did Beowulf do? What did his warriors do? What did Grendel do? What events occurred the next day? What reward did Beowulf receive? What new troubles arose in the night?* We were to answer these questions with one or two words or a short sentence. Occasionally Mr. Quennell would throw in a more involved question, to be answered in a couple of full sentences, but these were rare; they took too long to grade. His usual method of making his tests more challenging was not to ask harder or more complicated questions but rather to ask more of them. *How was Beowulf appealed to as the last resort? What did he ask for when he died? What did his funeral pyre look like? What was done with the treasure? What did some of Beowulf's men do?*

The class's grades on these tests were uniformly bad. The average score was 65 or 70, which was just passing. Some students never seemed to receive anything higher than 10 or 20. With a little scheming I managed to bring my own grades in line with the class average. Actually, this took less scheming than I had expected: Mr. Quennell was an unpredictable grader, and his reading of our tests was quirky. On one test he asked us where Grendel's attacks had taken place, and I gave as my answer the proper name of the mead hall the monster had terrorized. Mr. Quennell checked this wrong and wrote in the margin the answer he had been looking for: Denmark. On other occasions I earned low grades quite on my own, without any help from Mr. Quennell. This sometimes had unanticipated consequences. When I showed Ann a test on which I had earned a 42, she was horrified: "Forty-two!" she said. "You've got to do something about your grades!"

In a test on the General Prologue to the *Canterbury Tales,* I nearly gave myself away. The question was, "What was inscribed on the locket of the Prioress?" I wrote, "The letter A followed by '*Amor vincit omnia.*'" This is correct. But I later realized that the modernization we were using gave the proverb only in English, as something like "All surrender unto love." I worried all night that Mr. Quennell would wonder how I had happened to know the Latin. But he didn't. He just counted my answer wrong.

My answers weren't always wrong, though. Every now and then I managed to write something that pleased Mr. Quennell. The following sentences—my answer to the test question, "How is Beowulf shown to be Anglo-Saxon?"—earned me a "good" in the margin of my paper: "Beowulf is shown to be Anglo-Saxon by its Anglo-Saxon ideals. The ideals included courage which Beowulf always showed. Also a love of the sea which Beowulf and his men proved by coming to Denmark in a boat. Another is comitatus or loyalty which thanes showed by being loyal to the ring-givers or kings. When Beowulf gave gifts or when he got them he was giving an example of comitatus."

A high school teacher in another school who knew about my project told me before I enrolled at Bingham that my biggest problem would be writing tests and papers that would pass for twelfth-grade work. She said high school students nowadays write so poorly that virtually any adult posing as a student would give himself away immediately. Imitating the prose style of a modern high school student can indeed be a challenge. The key elements of that style, I discovered, are limited vocabulary, primitive syntax, lots of repetition, and no commas. Sentence fragments are a must. By the time I left I had mastered the basics and could produce sentences like "Plus it failed because he doesn't know it isn't" without batting an eye. I might have done even better, but I didn't get much practice: We almost never had to write.

Although we spent virtually all our time on *Beowulf* ("It's a great story—the best you'll ever read") and the first third of the *Canterbury Tales,* Mr. Quennell occasionally gave us more contemporary material for the sake of variety. Every couple of weeks he would pass around copies of *Scope,* a magazine for high school English students (consisting mostly of articles about TV stars), and we would spend a class period reading something that had caught his eye. One week we read a play called *House of Stairs,* which the editors of *Scope* described as being "in the tradition of *The Lord of the Flies.*" Here is an excerpt from the stage directions:

> The food machine is an important prop. It should look something like a Coke machine, and it requires a chute down which a prop person can roll food pellets. To achieve the blinking-light effect, someone can rapidly turn classroom lights on and off. To achieve the whispering-voices effect, a team of students can chant in unison.
>
> The time is the future. The place: a totalitarian country.

I don't know what it is about totalitarianism that fascinates high school English teachers. Mr. Quennell spoke of *1984* as though George Orwell shared a crypt with Shakespeare. His colleague Mr. Amberson taught a course called "The Contemporary Novel" whose reading list consisted of *Animal Farm, Fahrenheit 451,* and *Brave New World.* It may be that the literary values of the middle-aged majority of English teachers were irrevocably colored by the cold-war anxieties of their youth, to the continuing tedium of students everywhere. Matters of sensibility and style are maddeningly elusive—but *absolute dictatorial power,* there's something you can sink your teeth into. Or maybe the crucial consideration is simply that *Animal Farm, Fahrenheit 451,* and *Brave New World* all weigh in at under two hundred pages.

Another source of variety in Mr. Quennell's class was a

painfully dated essay by critic J. B. Priestley on the essence of English literature. Priestley's chauvinistic musings prompted Mr. Quennell to add a few thoughts of his own:

"You think you have some funny belt buckles now, but it was nothing compared to what they had in the Middle Ages."

"In Europe they had an academy. They set the rules: You must have eighteen words per sentence; you must have three paragraphs per page. I'm exaggerating a little. Characters in a tragedy must all act in one way. It was all very formalistic. But because England was an island, they didn't have any of those rules. They were very independent. They did it their own way."

"The English are really full of emotions, but they've learned to suppress it. And because they suppress it, they have to let it out sometimes. And when it comes out, it's very poetical."

"The English can be very humorous, but they're not just a kind of nice fat jolly ha-ha sort of people."

"Kings have to rely on the common people as volunteers for the army. The two most important things, army and money, they have to rely on other people for. This puts limitations on your monarchs."

"If I ask you on a test, 'Which English writer influenced the Russians?' what would you say? Dickens. What did Emily Brontë write about? The moors of Yorkshire. Who influenced Shakespeare? The Italians. Who influenced Chaucer? The French. If you can't remember that stuff you won't get anywhere."

"In Wales you wouldn't write about farms, would you? No, you would write about mountains, crags, and ridges. And in the Southeast you wouldn't write about mountains; you would write about beautiful rolling farm land, and cows, and the scenery. And up in the north sort of in the middle you would write about the lakes. England's got a lot of geography. We think we have a lot in this country, but it's nothing compared to England. How about Scotland? What would you write about there? The hardships of life."

Part Three

November

Do you remember a fragrance girls acquire in autumn? As you walk beside them after school, they tighten their arms about their books and bend their heads forward to give a more flattering attention to your words and in the little intimate area thus formed, carved into the clear air by an implicit crescent, there is a complex fragrance woven of tobacco, powder, lipstick, rinsed hair, and that perhaps imaginary and certainly elusive scent that wool, whether in the lapels of a jacket or the nap of a sweater, seems to yield when the cloudless fall sky like the blue bell of a vacuum lifts toward itself the glad exhalations of all things. This fragrance, so faint and flirtatious on those afternoon walks through the dry leaves, would be banked a thousandfold and lie heavy as the perfume of a flower shop on the dark slope of the stadium when, Friday nights, we played football in the city.

—John Updike

15
∾True Love

If the yearbook poll had been taken in the fall, the smart money at Bingham High School would have lined up behind Cathy Logan and Mark Lobrano for Best Couple. Without a doubt, they were the hottest, truest lovers in the school. You couldn't see one of them without wondering where the other one was, and when you saw the two of them together your mind virtually superimposed a little heart-shaped frame around their faces—the way you'd see them in the yearbook, along with the winners in the other categories of the poll. They were the hands-down all-stars, the uncontested champs. Even the teachers were swept along, kidding Cathy by calling her "Mrs. Lobrano" right in front of everyone, or razzing Mark about mortgage payments and nursery schools.

There was something about Mark and Cathy that set them apart, something that made them special. You would see them walking to school together every morning, crossing over the practice field and taking a swing past the wall in front of the New Wing, holding hands every step of the way. If they were early, Mark would follow Cathy to her homeroom, which was also mine, and they would shoot the breeze in a friendly, domestic way until the bell rang. Then Mark would give Cathy a quick peck on the lips and run for his own homeroom. Through the rest of the day they would meet between classes at preselected points around the school for a quick conversation or a fast french kiss.

Cathy was a compact blonde with big blue eyes and a nose that turned up right at the tip. Back in the eighth grade, when she and Mark started dating, she had a body that was going places, and now she was the Real Thing—not a cheerleader-type by any means, but a good-looking girl with long blond hair that crinkled a little, hippie-style. She wore faded bell-bottom blue jeans and billowy embroidered peasant blouses that looked like leftovers from the sixties. Mark was out of the same era, but with a touch of the hood thrown in. He was tall and gangly with long red hair and a dim mustache and goatee. He wore jeans and T-shirts and a denim jacket, along with a pair of motorcycle boots and a wallet that hooked onto his belt with a chain.

But Mark was no mere hood. He had some hoody friends and he liked to talk tough, but in general he was a laid-back character. Being in love had taken the kinks out of his pissed-off, rebellious soul. Cathy was his top priority; his hoody friends came second. This sometimes led to tensions—"Hey, Mark, ya wanna go trash some yards?" "Naw, I gotta help Cathy paint her room"—but that was just the way it was. Once the world starts to sink its hooks into you, you mellow out.

The only thing that kept Mark and Cathy from being the absolute top-dog deathless lovers of all time was the fact that they didn't live together. How could they? Their parents would have keeled over and died. So they did the next best thing: They shared a locker. The lockers at Bingham are standard split-level numbers with a long skinny compartment below for coats and gym clothes and a smaller, squarish compartment with its own door up above for books. There is only one hook in the lower compartment, so when Mark and Cathy moved in together, they had to put in an extra one so they could both hang up their stuff. They bought a big white plastic hook with a pressure-sensitive adhesive back and stuck it on the rear wall of the lower compartment. On the inside of the upper door they taped a picture of themselves, taken at a beach a summer or two before. Stuck to the door right next to the picture was a little plastic-coated magnet in the shape of a pineapple—the kind you see on refrigerators. When grades came out later in November, I saw Mark stick his report card to the door with the little magnet, so he'd remember to take it home, or maybe so Cathy would be sure to see it. Inside the compartment, along with their books, were cigarettes, matches, pens, pencils, a hairbrush, a comb, and a box of tampons.

The box of tampons was the crucial touch. More than anything else it stood for what Mark and Cathy felt about their love. It captured the essence of their utterly spontaneous, absolutely unfucked-up relationship. Being in love for them was not a crude novelty. It was just what they did. And the most thrilling thing about it was how *mundane* it all was. (Honey! Did you wash my jockstrap?) It was all old hat to them, this thing that the other kids were having cold sweats, dry heaves, and nervous breakdowns about. To the other kids Mark and Cathy seemed years older than they really were, and utterly composed, as though sex were no more out of the ordinary than a box of tampons in a locker.

Mark and Cathy were the greatest lovers at Bingham High School, but they weren't the only ones. There was also, for instance, Mike and Meredith, who were almost always bickering. I listened to one of their conversations at lunch:

"Why are you mad?" Meredith asked.

Mike said nothing.

"What's the matter? Did I do something?"

"I'm gonna quit that fuckin' job."

"What?"

"We're having a test in Data Processing that I just found out about."

"Is that what you're pissed about?"

"Yeah."

"And you're not pissed off at me?"

Mike said nothing.

"Well, are you?"

"I'm not gonna call 'em or nothin'. I'm just gonna not show up."

"Where do you work?" another boy asked. "Sears?"

"Stop & Shop," Mike said.

"I thought you worked at Sears."

"That don't start till fuckin' Friday."

"If you got another job, what are you so worried about?"

"I ain't worried about nothin'."

"Of course, if you quit, they'd fuck you over if you ever tried to get another job there."

"I would *never* do that. That place shits. I don't care what they do."

Meredith still looked worried. "Are you sure you aren't mad at me?" she asked after a long, uncomfortable silence. But still Mike said nothing.

Another day I saw Meredith in the "team room" of the gym. My gym class was coming back from its soccer game, and we had to pass through the team room to get to our lockers. Meredith was standing at the big blackboard the coaches used to diagram plays. She had filled the board almost completely with the round, sloping handwriting that is hereditary in high school girls. She was recording the names of all the couples she could think of: Howard and Jocelyn, Mary and Russell, Mimi and Don, Steve and Ruth, Kurt and Anne, Allan and Kay, Greg and Diane, Dick and Ginger, Jim and Melissa, Jim and Laura, Duncan and

Pam, Charlie and Jeanne, Andy and Sue, Bill and Peggy, and on and on. Each pair of names was enclosed in a squat, symmetrical heart.

I recognized a number of the names. Kurt and Anne were both in one of my classes, and I saw them every day, kissing, and sometimes more, in a little space between two banks of lockers in front of Mr. Bartlett's room. Steve and Ruth came to school early most mornings and spent fifteen minutes promenading arm in arm around the main part of the building. Kay and Allan spent most of their time writing each other notes that said things like "I don't think you understood what I meant the other day about when I said how I thought you never listened to what I said." Allan was always laboring over these communiqués and then handing them around for comments.

I noticed that a few couples I knew about were missing from Meredith's catalog, perhaps because they hadn't been going together long enough for Meredith to have found out about them. Like Bill Scalet and Amy Kendris.

Despite the fact that they had been friends since childhood, Bill and Amy had never been boyfriend and girl friend. Amy had always had other interests, and Bill was painfully shy around girls. In fact, he had never had a girl friend. But shortly after the sock hop, Amy and her Eisenhower boyfriend broke up, and she and Bill began to drift together. The early stages of their romance were so vague that they were noticeable only in retrospect. I think the beginning must have come one night very early in November. The gang was going to a movie (*Animal House*, again) and Bill talked Amy into driving. Amy had virtually the only car in Bill's circle of friends, a battered-up Buick Special with undependable steering and a perforated muffler. It wasn't much of a car, but for Bill and his friends it was an extremely important piece of machinery. After some persistent wheedling from Bill, Amy agreed to pick up all the kids and ferry them to the movie.

The night was important to me, because it was my first real evening out with my Bingham friends. Bill had invited me to join him and his friends on each of the two previous weekends, but I had declined both times; I was worried that I would give myself away. The closer I came to the kids in my class, the harder it would be to hide my real identity. I had been hoping to postpone most of my socializing until the very end of the semester, when it would make less difference if I were found out. I knew that once (or if) I became accepted as a real member of the gang, it would be difficult to extricate myself, and thinking about that made me nervous. Julia was nervous, too, but for a different reason: "How good a driver is this Amy Kendris person?"

Nervous or not, I couldn't put Bill off any longer without running the risk of being ostracized. So when he asked me, I told him I'd love to come to the movie. I did, however, take the precaution of meeting the other kids at the theater, rather than letting Amy pick me up; I didn't want my friends to get a very clear idea of where I "lived," for fear they might simply decide to drop by some night to see what I was up to. (A couple of weeks later, I found out, a few kids actually did drive by, but decided not to go in when they saw all the lights were out.)

At the movie that night, we all sat in the second row. Scott and Eric were there, and a girl from journalism named Michelle Champlin. Nothing very exciting happened, but about halfway through the movie, Bill and Amy got up to go to the concession stand and never came back. We later discovered they had moved to seats in the back of the theater. They said they were tired of leaning back to look at the screen. That was all there was to it, but looking back on it later I decided that in the theater that night must have been where their romance had begun. The rest of the night was uneventful, however. After the movie we went to Burger King for a hamburger and then decided not to try to buy some beer, not to smoke a joint that Scott had brought, and not to get up a poker game at Bill's house. So much for my big night out with the gang. When Amy took me home I had her drop me at the corner.

As time went by, Bill and Amy began to see more and more of each other. Amy started driving over to Bill's house after school or after work or after her night classes, and they would sit around in his room and shoot the breeze. Bill's room was a fairly typical teenager's room. I saw it several times when I went home with him after school. There was a poster on the back of the door that showed a skeleton sitting on a toilet saying, "When you gotta go, you gotta go." There was a Led Zeppelin poster over the bed and a couple of dusty old model airplanes on a shelf above the desk. When Amy came over, Bill's mom would hear her shot muffler about a block away and holler upstairs, "Hey, Bill, here she comes!" Then Bill would run around like a madman, straightening up his room and kicking his underwear under the bed. Sometimes Amy stayed for dinner and a little TV, and sometimes Bill went over to her house.

This new familiarity had a dramatic effect on Bill. He became much more bashful and reserved. I began to see him and Amy standing together outside the journalism classroom after fifth period. Amy wasn't in journalism, but her own class was right around the corner, so she and Bill had a little time to talk. Bill was so nervous at these meetings that he ducked his head way down to the point where his chin was virtually resting on his chest, and he stood there like that talking to Amy, not looking at her at all. If he happened to see me coming down the hall, he'd say, "Hey, Dave, what's happening?" and call me over for a little chat. Amy wasn't nervous in the least, but she told me she didn't mind having someone else there, because talking to Bill in the hall was frankly a bit of an ordeal.

"Amy used to go out with a college guy," Bill told me at lunch one day. "Some fucker about five years older than she was. I tell you, man, that chick is *sophisticated*."

I asked him if he had ever met Amy's latest boyfriend, the guy at Eisenhower High.

"Naw," he said, "but I get the impression he was a bit of a dip." Bill looked off into the distance. "Like he was crippled or something," he said vaguely, "or had half a brain. He had to talk by burping through a hole in his throat, you know, like all those old guys you always hear about. A real pathetic dude."

"How long did they go together?"

"Oh, I don't know," he said. "A couple of days."

"A couple of days?"

"Yeah, something. A few hours."

"She never even saw him in person," I suggested.

"That's the guy. They just wrote letters to each other." He paused. "Well, *he* wrote to *her*, anyway."

Bill and I had become pretty good friends in the weeks we had known each other. We goofed around in journalism and ate lunch together on Mondays, Wednesdays, and Fridays. Once we studied for a history test in the town library. We played basketball with some other guys after school, and we walked partway home together whenever we had the chance. He and Scott even invited me to go camping with them over Thanksgiving vacation. (I had to decline; Ann and I had already made plans for a trip.) But as Bill and Amy began to see more and more of each other, the invitations tapered off. When Bill and Amy went to movies now, it wasn't usually in a group. Their old friends didn't see as much of them as they used to. I felt a twinge of despair at this brotherly betrayal, as boys always do when one of their number falls in with a girl. But I also felt relieved, because the fact that Bill was now occupied elsewhere took some of the pressure off me. I didn't have to be on my toes quite so much.

Bill and Amy never really talked about what was going on between them, but one day before history I asked Bill how his weekend had been, and he flashed his big, bashful grin and said, "Great, really great." In case I had missed the point, he added, "Amy came over on Sunday and things are looking pretty good. Yeah, they're looking *pretty good.*"

I'm not exactly certain what Bill meant by "pretty good" when he told me about his weekend with Amy, but I do know one thing he didn't mean: He didn't mean that he and Amy were sleeping together. For the moment, anyway, the two of them were strictly small-time lovers, too shy to be very bold with each other.

Ever since the 1960s adults have imagined that teenagers everywhere are coupling and uncoupling with relative abandon. Teenagers are certainly freer about sex than they were twenty years ago, but changing societal attitudes have made the most difference for kids who probably would have had reasonably active sex lives anyway. The rich get richer. The new teenage state brought into being by the "sexual revolution" is by no means a democracy. People who didn't have much luck at sex as teenagers in 1960 wouldn't necessarily be having any more luck now. In fact, the sexual revolution makes life harder, not easier, for the rank and file. A boy whose bowels unhinge at the thought of kissing a girl will not be overjoyed by the news that he is now allowed (or expected) to take her to bed. The poor get poorer.

That doesn't mean that Bingham High School is a colony of virgins. A typical teenager's sex life has cooled off some since I was in high school (teenage lovers don't get the same kind of cultural reinforcement they did a decade ago) but there's still plenty going on. Steady couples that stay together long enough tend eventually to end up in bed. The free availability of birth control has eliminated most of the anxiety that was probably as formidable a barrier to sex as anything else. But for kids who don't already have boyfriends or girl friends, and who don't have much prospect of getting them, after-school relations with the opposite sex consist mostly of group activities, like our outings to the movies. Periodically these groups sort themselves out into steady pairs, but for most of the kids, "dating" is a communal activity. Public talk about sex is limited mostly to the wistful speculation that teenagers have always engaged in.

Teenagers like to complain that adults never understand how serious their love affairs are, but I suspect most adults do. Is there anything *more* serious than a teenage love affair? How many thirty-year-olds carve hearts in their furniture, or write their dates' or spouses' names on their clothes, or lie awake at four in the morning day after day composing unmailable notes to recalcitrant lovers? Ann sometimes kidded me that I ought to take advantage of my situation and find a teenage girl friend, but all things considered, who wouldn't rather have a wife?

16
∂ "A Witness to History"

Early in November, Iranian militants captured the American embassy in Teheran and took its fifty-three occupants hostage. A few days later, in psychology, Mr. Chapin said, "If they harm one hair on one head of one American over there, I'm in favor of unleashing our atomic arsenal and turning the whole Middle East into one giant oil well. They'll be swimming in camels instead of riding on 'em." The next day, Mr. Bartlett, my history teacher, gave us a lecture on the same topic. History was one of three classes Bill Scalet and I had together. Bill's desk was up near Mr. Bartlett's. Mine was in the back row. When the bell rang and Mr. Bartlett, a great big man who had played football in college, poured himself a cup of coffee from his Thermos, Bill put his head down on his desk and closed his eyes. Nap time.

Mr. Bartlett pulled down one of his big spring-loaded wall maps and pointed out the Islamic countries from the west coast of Africa to the Pacific Ocean. "It's a big world, folks," he said, "and it's easy to forget that the United States, in terms of population, is a pretty small fraction of it." He shifted gears and began to speak generally about political responsibility and power. Did we realize, he asked, that the students holding the embassy in Teheran were not much older than we were? He talked about the frustrations of adolescence and how they are occasionally translated into political action, sometimes with global consequences. He mentioned the student protests of the sixties and early seventies.

Dawn Lavin, who had a bloodhound's nose for extra credit, piped up: "Did I tell you about the statewide church retreat I went on last week, Mr. Bartlett? We elected our own governor and a senate and a house of representatives."

Mr. Bartlett, caught virtually in midsentence, smiled wearily and shook his head. He was so patient he'd have made a nun feel pushy. But he also knew how to hold his ground. Before Dawn could think of anything else to say, he had picked up where he left off.

"I don't mean to sound alarmist or anything, but you kids should know that if a war resulted from the events now taking place in the Middle East, you would be the ones to fight it. You owe it to yourselves and to the rest of us to have some understanding of what goes on in the world. Armies depend for their existence on the very young, the seventeen-, eighteen-, nineteen-year-olds. Kids at that age are at the peak of their physical powers, and, what's more, they're more willing than anybody else to fight and even die. You kids feel a lot of frustration for social and biological reasons that don't have much to do with political struggles, but the fact is that politicians can and do take advantage of those frustrations and desires."

This was a familiar theme with Mr. Bartlett. Not long before, he had given us a handout listing the seven forms of propaganda: "Card Stacking, Plain Folks, Band Wagon, Name Calling, Testimonial, Transfer, and Glittering Generality." Recent events had made that handout seem particularly timely.

"Why don't we just bomb Iran?" Mike Sperling, president of the student council, asked.

Mr. Bartlett shrugged. "You tell me," he said. "Is that the way you think we ought to handle this situation? This isn't just a hypothetical case, you know. There are people in the government who are asking the same question."

He paused for our reaction. There was none. Bill Scalet was snoozing. Dawn Lavin was chatting audibly with a girl sitting next to her. The consensus in our class was that Mr. Bartlett was nice but boring, with too many personal opinions. Bill told me once that Mr. Bartlett was a good guy, one of the best, but a complete and total drag as a teacher.

Bill and Mike weren't the only student leaders in Mr. Bartlett's class. Two of Bingham's four National Merit Letter of Commendation winners were there, along with the captain of the girls' volleyball team, the girl with the highest grade-point average in the school, two senior class officers, and a couple of kingpins from the football team.

Now Mr. Bartlett was gearing up again, trying a new approach to the issues he was addressing.

"What would you say," he asked, "has been the single most important political event in the world in the last fifteen years?"

There was a long silence. Mr. Bartlett looked from face to face around the room. Finally Mike Sperling took a stab at an answer: "World War Two?"

Mike Sperling knows the political scene at Bingham High School backwards and forwards. In his three years at Bingham he's held all the positions worth holding: president of his class both sophomore and junior years, now president of the student council. He is six feet tall and has an average build and average looks; his muddy blond hair curls up over the tops of his ears, but just barely. He wears a sterling-silver ID bracelet engraved with the name of his girl friend, Ellen, a junior at another school. In addition to a traditional blue three-ring binder for his schoolwork, he carries a sleek black vinyl "Organizer" bulging with the minutes of innumerable meetings. On days when the student council convenes, he wears a tie. He looks like a campaigner. When he stands up to make an announcement in assembly, you're halfway surprised that Ellen isn't there beside him, smiling, waving, and playing the candidate's wife.

Mike Sperling isn't running for anything, however. What he wants to do when he gets out of high school is to go to a college like Colorado State or the University of New Mexico, log a little heavy play time, and then go into business. "Business is where all the money is," he told me, convincingly, one day before history. I had asked him whether he thought he would ever run for public office. "There's no percentage in being in government," he said. "Your hands are tied. It's the businessmen who have all the real power. I want to get a master's in business and then make a pile working for a corporation with a future. Like Exxon."

There's no reason why Mike ought to want to go into politics, of course. Student council presidents aren't necessarily born politicians. Some of them turn out to be grocery store managers, or lawyers, or washing machine repairmen, or newspaper reporters. Or even high school teachers. In fact, one day when Mr. Bartlett was at home with the flu, the substitute who filled in for him was a young man who had been president of the student council at Eisenhower High School in 1972. His name was David Barber. He was tall and frail looking, had long blond hair, and wore wire-rimmed glasses. When he stood before our class that day, he was awkward and nervous. He wanted us to like him, but he didn't get off to a very good start. Mr. Bartlett had left him a list of assignments, and he was having trouble making it out. He handed the sheet to a girl sitting near his desk to see if she could decipher it. He brushed his hair out of his eyes and smiled.

It took the class about five seconds to come to the conclusion that David Barber was a pushover. Michelle and Dawn moved their desks together so they could talk more easily. Eddie Wyzanski went to get something from his locker without asking. Mike Sperling opened a big cardboard box on his desk and asked if anyone wanted to buy student council candy.

Mr. Barber perked up. "Oh," he said, "are you on the student council?"

"Yeah," Dawn said, "he's the president."

"No kidding?" Mr. Barber said. "I was stuco president at Eisenhower when I was there. We had a pretty radical organization that year. We made a lot of big reforms. How about you guys? Do you have a powerful council?"

Mike shrugged. The substitute was making him, and everyone else, uncomfortable. There was his hair, for one thing. And those glasses: round. "Anybody got change for a dollar?" Mike asked.

Mr. Barber walked over to Mike's desk. He had gone into teaching, he said, because he had decided when he graduated that all the best possibilities for making a difference in the world were in the field of education. His experience on the student council, among other things, had made him optimistic about making some genuine reforms that would go beyond the school system to society itself.

"We forced the administration to change the whole schedule," he said. "We made them get rid of homeroom first thing in the morning. When you went to school you went straight to your first-period class. Then after first period there was a four-minute homeroom just to take attendance. And it was all the council's idea."

"Didn't a lot of kids cut first period?" Mike asked.

"No," Mr. Barber said. "That was the great thing. There was no problem at all. Absolutely none." He looked around the room triumphantly and then turned back to Mike. "What kind of stuff do you guys do? On the council, I mean."

"They sell candy," Michelle said.

"Why candy?"

"To pay for dances, duh," Dawn said.

"How did you pay for *your* dances?" Mike asked.

Mr. Barber looked genuinely puzzled. "The student council didn't have any dances," he said. "We didn't even have a prom that year."

"No prom?"

"How queer!"

"I can't believe it!"

"I told you," Mr. Barber said. "It was a pretty radical bunch. The class voted not to have a prom because it was too decadent."

"I can't believe it!"

"Gross!"

Mike looked at him contemptuously for several seconds. "So," he said, "do you want some M&Ms or not?"

"The young and the old," Mr. Bartlett told us one day, "are two potentially powerful blocs of voters that politicians in recent years have been appealing to. When the voting age was lowered from twenty-one to eighteen, it was thought—feared— that the eighteen-to-twenty-one-year-olds would be able to sway elections. Numerically, it's more than possible. But it hasn't happened, because only about ten percent of the eighteen-year-olds who are registered to vote actually vote. And that's just the ones who register. The overall percentage would be much lower, of course."

"I'm going to vote," someone said.

"Senior citizens, on the other hand, have had some real success in organizing themselves. These are people in forced retirement, people living in inferior subsidized housing, people living on fixed incomes. This is an area that Senator Kennedy, among other people, has been very active in. Senior citizens have even formed their own activist group—it's called the Gray Panthers."

Everybody laughed.

"What do they do," Bill Scalet asked, "ride around in their wheelchairs bashing people over the head with their canes?"

"Believe it or not," Mr. Bartlett said, "these issues will be important to you someday. People live longer than they used to, and they stay healthy longer. Old people in good shape don't think they should have to retire from their jobs just because they've reached the age of sixty-five or seventy. Meanwhile, the young people, who are in a hurry to get started on their own lives and careers, want the old people to step aside."

"That's right," a boy said.

"Euthanasia," Bill said.

There was more laughter.

"Of course," Mr. Bartlett continued, "the ones who *really* have it tough are those of us who are in between. It sure is hard to be twenty-two. . . ."

"Ha ha ha."

"How old *are* you, Mr. Bartlett?"

"I'll give you a hint. The year I was born a great tyrant invaded two countries and precipitated a huge war."

"That's not fair."

"Too tough for you?" Mr. Bartlett said. "I'll give you another hint. It was at the end of the Great Depression."

"Fifty."

"I said the *end* of the Great Depression."

"Fifty-five."

"Holy cow," Mr. Bartlett said.

"Forty."

"Wait," he said. "Hold on. Did one of you geniuses say forty? I'm thirty-nine."

Like a lot of high school teachers, Mr. Bartlett is obsessed with time. Every September he is a year older, while the students are always the same age: sixteen, seventeen, eighteen. A teacher can almost hear time passing. He tries to joke about it with the kids. "That was back in the days of my youth," Mr. Chapin said one day, "you know, when Moses was parting the Red Sea." "We used to have a pet dinosaur at my folks' house," Mr. Bartlett said. "That was back in the Stone Age," Mr. Amberson said, "when I was a little boy." "You've probably read about my father," Mr. Pottle said. "He was the guy who invented the wheel."

When Mr. Bartlett came to Bingham High School he was a young man, just out of college, on his way to bigger and better things. He kept meaning to move on to a university professorship, but somehow he never did. He told us one day that over the years he had accumulated close to one hundred hours of graduate work toward his Ph.D., many of them at an Ivy League university. He has taken several leaves of absence to work on his dissertation, but for one reason or another he has always returned. He has a wife and a couple of kids and it's too late for him to go running around the country looking for a better job. The hot young comer of fifteen years ago has become the grand old man of the social studies department.

High school kids have their own ways of measuring time. The day is divided not into hours but into periods. Students don't say, "See you at two," they say, "See you after seventh." The divisions of the school year exaggerate the divisions of the natural year. A teenager's sense of changing seasons has a precision that fades after graduation. Summer is something

tangible, a definite, particular piece of time squared off at either
end by the boundaries of semesters. Autumn is doubly poignant:
The death of the green world and the beginning of the school
year are parallel events. Each season has its own sports, its own
vacations, its own activities. Every textbook is a calendar; every
year is four report cards long; every hour that passes is marked
by the ringing of a bell. Every class is named for a moment in
time: the class of 1980, the class of 1981. Spring brings the
promise not only of natural renewal but also, for a student, of
liberation.

For a teacher, time collapses into itself. A teacher reads the
same books at the same rate year after year. He cracks the same
jokes. He looks into the same faces and listens to the same
questions, no matter that the names change. The distance
between him and his pupils is anchored only at one end, the low
end. For most of the rest of us, aging is less palpable; the people
we work with grow older as we do. Teachers grow older at
accelerated rates.

"You talk big now about how you hate school and how you
can't wait to be out in the real world," Mr. Amberson told us one
morning in homeroom. "But you'll see. You'll be just like the rest
of them. Once you get out, you'll be trying to get back. They
won't be able to keep you away from the building. You'll be
mooning around and saying these were the best years of your
lives." For a teacher, the enemy is time.

Mr. Bartlett, clearly, believes that he is running out of time.
But the fact that he has remained at Bingham High School all
these years is proof that to a certain extent he has surrendered
to it. He has carved himself a niche in time. His enemy is also
his ally. If he has given up something by remaining a high
school teacher, he has also gained, because in a high school, as
in few other places, he can be a grand old man at the age of
thirty-nine. He doesn't have to fight for a place, and he doesn't
have to pit himself against any really worthy rivals—at least
not a university full of them. And so the dissertation drags on,

and the book is never written, and the doctorate never quite falls into place.

Mr. Bartlett is a kind of teacher I don't think can be found many places *but* in a high school. He is also one of the small handful of really great teachers I have ever had—this in spite of the fact that most of his students find him boring. There is something just a little bit tragic about him that gives him a real nobility in a classroom. He is absolutely without cynicism. I believed him when he said he wept when the extent of the Watergate scandal first became clear. He viewed Richard Nixon's behavior in the White House as a personal insult, an affront to his own dignity.

"I think this country is facing some very serious problems right now," Mr. Bartlett told us one day at the end of a long discussion about political corruption, "but you're not going to do anything about them by doing what I'm doing: preaching. Preaching can turn you off just as much as turn you on." Actually, Mr. Bartlett preaches very little. The most impressive thing about him is his patience. He doesn't berate students who are wrong or with whom he disagrees, he simply keeps expanding the discussion by bringing up new points until he has assembled a comprehensive picture bit by bit. He cares intensely about his subject and takes pride in lecturing without notes, with every name, date, and figure committed to memory. When he lectures I sometimes have the feeling he is addressing not so much his students as himself. He is trying to reassure himself about the things he believes, using us to test his faith. I find it all very stirring, although I admit I am distinctly in the minority. Most of the other kids take him at his word, accepting his description of himself as a "preacher," a man full of ideas.

The ideas of a high school teacher have a tendency to become a little eccentric—teenagers aren't much of an obstacle to a fertile imagination—and Mr. Bartlett has eccentricities. He shares what I think is a common belief among civics teachers, that what is wrong with things in general is that they are *irrational*:

people are wasteful, committees are inefficient, states have nongeometric shapes, people who don't know how to use the mimeograph machine try to use it anyway, textbooks are arranged incoherently (he loves outlines). Over the years he has developed what amounts to his own textbook, an impressive library of mimeographed pages, which he distributes periodically through the year. My notebook is filled to overflowing with them: selections from the *Federalist Papers*; an analysis of the way political parties operate; a general outline of the key events in American history from 1918 to the present; a copy of a government brochure on what to do in a voting booth; an article from a political journal describing positions taken by the current candidates for president; a map showing the congressional districts in our state; a paragraph-by-paragraph guide to the Constitution of the United States; a detailed description of how bills are passed in the House and Senate; a list of study hints, including his "seven questions," WHO, WHAT, WHEN, WHERE, HOW, WHY, and SO WHAT?

Mr. Bartlett's inability to spark the imaginations of most of his students probably arises from the very qualities I find most admirable: his patience, his doubts about governments, his careful approach to large philosophical questions. Students don't like teachers who can't make up their minds. I once asked half a dozen (non-Bingham) high school students what qualities they thought distinguished a good teacher from an ordinary or a bad one. A good teacher, they more or less agreed, "has control of the class," "can discipline well," "keeps everything under control," "knows how to talk to you" (i.e., like somebody else's parent), "gets the message across," and so on. However much they may complain on the side, teenagers feel most comfortable with teachers who are essentially authoritarians. Self-doubt makes them nervous (they feel too much of it themselves). Despite his enormous physical presence, Mr. Bartlett puts across a weakness in class that diminishes his students' respect for him.

Perhaps Mr. Bartlett thinks too highly of us, or expects too much. When we have tests he routinely leaves the classroom for five or ten minutes at a time, to rinse out his coffee cup or run off a few handouts on the mimeograph machine. During these unsupervised periods, cheating is rampant. Almost everyone does it. Even the most intelligent, responsible kids begin discussing the questions on the tests in near-normal voices the instant Mr. Bartlett is safely out of the room. Every time we have a test, he goes away. It's almost as though he's doing it on purpose. I talked about this once with Bill. "It almost seems like he's doing it to give people a chance to cheat," I said. But Bill said, "No, man, it isn't that; Mr. Bartlett just trusts everybody; he wants us to know that he respects us."

"This isn't a subject," Mr. Bartlett told us one day. "This isn't a course. It's the future of mankind. What are you going to do? This is reality, folks. We're talking about your lives."

Mr. Bartlett had been talking about Congress and civil rights. He started out with a brief discussion of parliamentary procedure, then moved on to the civil rights movement. He told us about the Civil Rights Act of 1960, about growing dissatisfaction among blacks in the South, and about early victories and defeats in the fight against discrimination. He explained President Kennedy's postelection vacillation about the major civil rights legislation he had promised in his campaign. He told us about the assassination of Medgar Evers, George Wallace's "standing in the schoolhouse door," and the March on Washington for Jobs and Freedom. He moved on to the Civil Rights Bill of 1964, its quick and overwhelming passage in the House and the subsequent battle and filibuster in the Senate. The filibuster, he said, lasted more than two months. It was ended on June 10, 1964, by a vote of cloture that few had expected to be successful.

"I was in Washington during the final weeks of the filibuster," he told us. "I decided for once to be a witness to history. I was over there at the Senate every single day, and I can tell you for a fact, it was a frightening, exciting time."

Mr. Bartlett was lecturing, as usual, without notes, leaning against the front of his desk. "The petition for cloture was filed on June eighth, and the vote was scheduled for eleven a.m. on June tenth, which was a Wednesday. I had been up and in line at the Capitol every morning at four o'clock, to get a seat in the visitors' gallery. The public is allowed to go in and watch, but there's only a limited amount of space, and they dole it out on a first-come-first-served basis. So I went early every day, and on Thursday I stayed to watch the last hours of the filibuster.

"By one a.m. I was the only visitor left. Senator Robert Byrd of West Virginia, one of the southern Democrats, was at the podium. He was reading articles from the newspaper and his wife's recipes and that sort of thing. Just whatever came into his head. Senator Richard Russell of Georgia, another Democrat, who was the leader of the bloc of southern senators, was there in case Byrd faltered. Every time Byrd cleared his throat or yawned or scratched his fanny, Russell hopped up out of his seat. Senator Brewster, who was the acting president of the Senate, was there, too, snoring away. Roger Mudd was alone in the press gallery. The five of us were the only ones there in that big, empty, solemn hall, and the only sound was Byrd droning along and Brewster sawing wood, hour after hour."

Mr. Bartlett told us about the cloture vote the next day, and about how it passed narrowly He told us that Hubert Humphrey did a little dance, and Everett Dirksen thumbed his nose at Barry Goldwater. And he told us about the vote on the actual bill, which came on June 19

"The opposition was futile,' he said. "The final tally was seventy-three to twenty-seven in favor. Senator Charles Weltner of Georgia, who had formerly been against, voted in favor. When he cast his vote he said something I later memorized: 'Change, swift and certain, is upon us, and we in the South face some difficult decisions. We can offer resistance and defiance, with their harvest of strife and tumult. We can suffer continued demonstrations, with their wake of violence and disorder. Or we can acknowledge this measure as the law of the land. We can accept the verdict of the nation. I will add my voice to those who seek reasoned and conciliatory adjustment to a new reality.'

"It was a brave position and, certainly, a great victory. The Civil Rights Act was a supremely important piece of legislation, perhaps the most important of your lifetimes. You owe it to yourselves and to your country to understand it. When it was all over I let out a whoop and ran out of the gallery to call my wife."

17
℘ "Stinks and Boring"

Even though Bill Scalet didn't listen very carefully in history, he would have been the first to admit that a lot of his ideas for the editorials he wrote came from Mr. Bartlett. Bill hung around in Mr. Bartlett's classroom during free periods and after school, helping him staple mimeographed handouts or simply chewing the fat. However much he might complain about Mr. Bartlett's boring lectures, Bill idolized the man and talked about him often. "Once," he told me, "two guys were fighting in the hall, really trying to fuck each other up, and Mr. Bartlett came out and grabbed both guys by the front of their shirts and lifted them right off the ground against the lockers. Man, those guys were shaking." Mr. Bartlett also listened to Bill's gripes about journalism and tried to help him when he couldn't think of anything to write about.

It was one of these bull sessions that gave Bill the idea for his editorial about boat people, the starving refugees who were fleeing Vietnam in leaky vessels and perishing in astounding numbers in the South China Sea. He labored over the piece for days and handed it in to Mrs. Griswold. In accordance with her policy of treating the kids in her class as a team of reporters, she read the editorial and then passed it around to a couple of the other kids for comments.

"Stinks and boring," one girl wrote in the margin of the first page. Bill was irate. The editorial was a long, emotional appeal for an international relief effort to aid the refugees. To drive home the point, Bill described some children, "splashing and gurgling in the middle of the ocean, their cries drowned out by waves crashing on their heads." Bill was really proud of that image—it seemed to put the whole situation in a nutshell—but not many of the other kids liked it. When the editorial came up for discussion, Sheila McNichols, one of five cheerleaders in the class, said the "splashing and gurgling" part was too gross. Mrs. Griswold agreed, more or less, and deleted it. It didn't matter that Bill was coeditor, because Mrs. Griswold had final say about what went into the paper and what didn't. Bill felt betrayed.

In addition to his long, serious editorials, Bill liked to write short, funny, irreverent pieces that he thought would liven up the paper. One of these was a sort of parody of the "Point/ Counterpoint" routines that Jane Curtin and Dan Aykroyd were always doing on *Saturday Night Live. Saturday Night Live* was everybody's favorite show, and it was the source of a lot of the humor at Bingham High. Bill's parody followed the form pretty closely. It started out, "Jane, you ignorant slut," just the way the routines always did on TV, and then it went on to talk about the lunches at Bingham and how terrible they were. Bill couldn't reread his parody without falling into hysterics. But Mrs. Griswold was not impressed. "I think it's wonderful that you are so inventive," she said, "but I don't think this kind of language belongs in a newspaper." Sheila McNichols, among others, agreed.

Bill was terribly upset. It seemed to him that he couldn't even get an article printed in his own newspaper. He was mad at Mrs.

Griswold and mad at Sheila McNichols, and pretty soon he started writing short little pieces that began, "Mrs. Griswold, you ignorant slut." He didn't hand these in, of course, he just showed them to friends. Pretty soon lots of the guys in the class were writing them, and they all started the same way, although some of them began, "Sheila, you ignorant slut." One day one of these fell into the hands of one of the cheerleaders, who promptly turned it over to Mrs. Griswold. Bill got into more trouble over that than he had been in yet, and Mrs. Griswold began talking about stripping away some of his editorial responsibilities. "Some of you," she said, "have not been making an effort. The Publications Office this morning was a mess. There were materials all over the place, there were scissors left out and pica rulers, and the stack of old papers was a *mess*. Sometimes I wonder if you kids even care. But this is your paper. I'm not going to do all the work for you. If you don't want to buckle down and do it, then fine, we won't put out a paper. Lord knows, it's expensive to publish."

"There wouldn't be any problem if we'd just publish the stuff we have," Bill muttered.

Mrs. Griswold didn't hear this. "*Some* of you are lazy and disobedient. *Some* of you waste class time doing things you have no business doing. *Some* of you are consistently late coming up from lunch. And it's the same people every day. Some of you who do not fulfill your duties as editors may find one day that you are no longer editors."

Bill's "Point/Counterpoint" parodies and the perpetual mess in the Publications Office weren't the only things that were bothering Mrs. Griswold. The newspaper's printer had just raised his prices five dollars a page, the first increase in fifteen years. Even though the cost was still quite low—about $325 for the usual run of one thousand six-page papers—it was getting harder and harder to make ends meet. Every member of the staff was supposed to put in at least a little time selling ads (at about a dollar a column-inch) but almost no one did. There was a little extra income from special advertisements, but Mrs. Griswold charged so little for these that they didn't make much difference; a dozen members of the staff spent more than an hour stuffing a preprinted supplement into all one thousand copies of the first edition of the year, a service for which the advertiser paid ten dollars.

Most of the *Bomber*'s revenues, apart from a stipend paid by the school, came from single-copy sales. On the day the paper came out, we were all supposed to come to school early and spend a quarter of an hour before homeroom hawking papers in the halls at twenty-five cents apiece. Bill, Scott and several others found this so demeaning that they would give away copies to friends and then kick in a couple of dollars each out of their own pockets. Two papers were published in the time I was at Bingham. I don't think we sold more than two hundred copies of either. Boxes of unsold, unread newspapers stacked up under the work tables in the Publications Office.

Since the newspaper's readership was small and, apparently, dwindling, Bill may have decided that it didn't matter whether his articles appeared or not. As time went by he spent more and more of his time in journalism working on funny stories and letters that were not intended for publication. One of these purported to be a note from Mrs. Griswold to Sheila McNichols:

> *Dear Butiful Miss McNichols:*
>
> *I have been observing you for some time and know that you think you are better than any one else in the class just because you are a cheerleader. I have just about had it with you cheerleaders. Your always making trouble in this class and hugging eachother and sitting on your laps and poking eachothers boobs. What are you lesbiens? No one else can work when your showing off. You are not even very good*

*cheerleaders and you and some of your friends are to
fat. Your behavior makes it difficult for the other
students to work when you are acting like homos no
one els can concentrait.*

Mrs. Griswold

Sheila McNichols, a.k.a. "McNipples," was a tall cheerleader
with a fervent following in the backfield of the football team.
She had Farrah-cut black hair, dimples in both cheeks, and eyes
that were almost always half-closed under the weight of her
long, long lashes. She wore inexpensive wraparound dresses and
tight designer jeans, and sometimes she let a little cleavage
show. All of which is to say that, except for the fact that she was
a certified hot number, Sheila bore a strong resemblance to the
other girls in the class.

By virtue of her superior looks, however, Sheila could get
away with things the other girls couldn't. Sometimes, though,
her looks got her into trouble. It was fifth period, journalism
class. Bill and a couple of other (male) members of the newspaper staff had gone down to the darkroom shared by Bingham's
newspaper and yearbook to scrounge for photographs. The
deadline for the current issue was approaching fast, and Bill
had lots of space to fill.

"You won't believe what I've got," Carl Morgan, the photo
editor, said when all of us were inside. He flicked on the light
and pulled a picture out of a tray of chemicals. "I took it this
morning," he said. "Isn't it incredible?"

What it was was a head shot of Sheila McNichols, taken from
too low and too close to her face. Her nostrils were black and
gaping. Her chin looked like a softball. Her hair was pulled back
behind her ears, and her forehead shone. Flat lighting had
eliminated the contours of her face, making her cheeks look
round and fat.

"It's the most beautiful picture I've ever seen," Bill said. He had been itching for a chance to get back at Sheila and her friends. The phony letters had boosted his spirits, but they weren't completely satisfying. Lately Bill had been referring to the cheerleaders as "my elves," because they always seemed to be wearing their purple-and-gold uniforms, always giggling and goosing each other, always tinkering on the paper with tiny elfin tools—and never paying any attention to him, except to criticize something he had written. These criticisms had a frightening sexual edge to them, and most of the other boys could feel it, too. The cheerleaders were just an overwhelming presence in the class; you could almost reach out and grab the sexual frustration. They made the boys fretful and the other girls nervous. Sometimes the captain of the football team would drop by on his way to somewhere else, and one of the cheerleaders would throw her arms around him, or make him pretend to sit in her lap, or try to get a hold on the waistband of his underpants and pull. And all of this set off some very mean vibrations.

"I think this is perhaps the single most important photograph ever taken," Bill said.

"Better put it back in the fixer, Bill," Carl said. "If you don't leave it in long enough, it'll turn yellow."

"Is there any way to do it with the fixer so just the teeth turn yellow?" We were all cackling with glee.

"Well, I guess we could try. . . ."

"We could do another print of just the teeth, and not put them in the fixer for very long, and then glue those teeth over the real ones."

"This is the ugliest picture I ever saw."

"Gentlemen, the camera does not lie."

"Put a bag over her head!"

"Let's blow that nose way up, Carl. I want to take a look inside those pores."

"We could make Halloween masks out of this and then all wear them on Halloween."

"The police would never stand for it."

"Let's have a few wallet-sized, Carl."

"I want to put it on one of those T-shirts with pictures."

"You should have gotten her bending over so we could have had a picture of her fat little ass."

"It would have broken the lens!"

"We could blow this way up and stick it in the window in the Publications Office with Super Glue and then lock the door. Nobody would be able to get it off."

Bill's eyes opened wide. "Shit, man, we ought to print up about a hundred of these damn things and stick 'em up all over the school!"

Half an hour later, while the rest of us were at lunch, Bill took two of the very worst pictures, signed each, "With love to Bingham High School, the Wicked Witch of the West," and put them up in two stairwells. When the crowds surged up the stairs after lunch, the pictures were right there on the walls, large as life. You couldn't avoid them. The cheerleaders were furious, of course, but they left the pictures up until sometime later, when Sheila found out about them and tore them down. She vowed revenge, but she had no way of proving who had done it, so nobody got in trouble. Bill told me he felt as though he had received a stay of execution.

As anyone who has participated in extracurricular activities knows, one of the best things about being on a team or acting in a play or working on a publication is the privilege such a position entails. You get to prowl around in parts of the school that other students never see. You are allowed to leave classes for special events. You get to know at least a few of your teachers in a more informal way than is ordinarily possible. On my old high school newspaper we used to fill idle moments plotting elaborate pranks designed to infuriate the humorless principal and his equally humorless lieutenants: an indoor invitational golf tournament (eighteen holes around the halls), the Great Chair Heist (we stole all the chairs in the high school building and locked them in the newspaper office), meticulously planned raids against the yearbook office (which was next door to ours and accessible through a loose panel in the ceiling).

Journalism students at Bingham were among the most privileged in the school; we were all issued press passes, which entitled us to be in the halls without supervision if we were working on assignments, and even to leave the building if we needed to sell ads or deliver copy to the printer. Of course, high school privileges are made to be abused, and we all took advantage of our special status. Most of the kids did no work at all unless there was an issue to put out, and since the paper was published only six times a year, there was seldom much pressure to get things done. Every so often Mrs. Griswold would crack down and give us a bawling out, but most of the time she let things drift.

When we did have a newspaper to put out, the pace quickened a little, although even then the staff was laconic. Articles were assigned by Mrs. Griswold with the help of the two news editors, Keith Edwards and Susan Melandy. The first step was to comb through the corresponding numbers from previous years and reassign every story that was still even remotely newsworthy. As a result, there was a certain sameness to the issues from one year to the next. The front page of virtually every first paper for a decade had included stories headlined BINGHAM WELCOMES NEW TEACHERS, FACULTY PLAY PLANNED, BINGHAM STUDENT ACHIEVES HONORS ON STATE EXAM, BINGHAM WELCOMES AFS STUDENT. Wording and even placement were nearly identical, and entire paragraphs were lifted, where possible, from earlier stories. This made reading the paper a bit tedious to old-timers, but it lightened the reporters' load considerably and gave us more time to do what we liked to do best, which was nothing. I had to work a little harder on my own assignment, since there had never been an article about a financial-aid conference before, but even so I didn't have much space to fill. Here's my story, as it finally appeared (I didn't get a byline):

CONFERENCE SLATED FOR FINANCIAL AID

The Guidance Department is sponsoring a Financial Aid Conference for all eleventh and twelfth grade students and their parents at 7 pm Nov. 6 in BHS auditorium.

A guest speaker will make a presentation and then a representative of the Guidance Department will talk to parents about the various kinds of scholarships.

"I get the feeling that the parents and students really appreciate the information they receive," noted Guidance Counselor Mrs. Collier.

Nothing special, maybe, but I was pleased with it at the time. The only change Mrs. Griswold made was to insert the word "noted" in the last sentence where I had written "said," a correction which toned up my article considerably.

Bill's budding romance with Amy had improved his outlook a great deal. He still liked to make trouble in class, but his running feud with the cheerleaders slackened as his love affair bolstered his confidence. Sometimes, though, his love life suffered reverses. I learned about a setback at one of the after-school basketball games the boys on the staff held occasionally at a public playground up the road from the school. During a break in the action, Bill told me that he had been asked to the Winter Cotillion, a semiformal dance that would be held just before Christmas vacation, and that he didn't know what to do about it.

"Don't you want to go?" I asked.

"Sure, man, I guess."

"Then what's the problem?"

"I want to go with *Amy*."

"It wasn't Amy who asked you?"

"No, man, that's the thing. It was Mary Humbert." Mary was a girl in our English class.

"What did you tell her?" I asked.

"I said I'd go with her if Amy didn't ask me later."

"Very smooth."

"I didn't know what else to do. I really want to go with Amy."

"What did Amy say?"

"I haven't asked her about it." He shook his head. "Man, I'm screwed."

"Maybe you'd better tell Amy."

"I was gonna, man, but I don't want to put any pressure on her."

"Then you're stuck."

"I guess so. Christ, this really sucks."

"Doesn't Mary know that you and Amy are going out?"

"Sure, I think. I don't know why she did it."

"Maybe she wants to steal you away from Amy."

"Yeah, that's it. All the chicks are hot after my ass."

"Maybe you should hold out until you see if Sheila will ask you."

"*Highly* likely." He thought for a moment. "Hey, why don't *you* go with Mary."

I wasn't sure how to respond to this. "I don't know," I said. "Maybe she wouldn't want to go with me."

"Yeah, probably not."

I let this pass. Bill spent the next week in a state of nervous despair before finally finding the nerve to mention the problem to Amy. She took charge immediately and smoothed things over with Mary. Mary, it turned out, hadn't been aware that Amy and Bill were serious about each other. This wasn't surprising, considering how inconspicuous their romance was. The jilted Mary, meanwhile, found another date. If I was ever in the running for that position, I never heard about it.

Julia was upset when she heard I'd been passed over. "Somebody ought to call that girl's mother," she said.

18
∾ Fearful Symmetry

The casual after-school basketball games organized by the boys in journalism were fun and even lively, but they were hardly the state of the art as far as that sport was concerned. *Real* basketball at Bingham was played by black students. When the basketball season got underway in November, only one white student, a guard, tried out. An assistant coach referred to him amiably as "the short white hope." Ten years before, there had been no blacks on the Bingham High School team.

The racial transformation of basketball at Bingham is not an isolated phenomenon; similar changes have taken place at schools all over the country. Nor is the change merely a matter of the color of the players' skin; underlying it is a change in society as a whole.

The legacy of the civil rights movement does not hang heavy over Bingham High School. The blacks in the student body were four and five and six years old when Martin Luther King was assassinated. The principal figures of the civil rights movement are in many ways as remote to them as they are to their white classmates. Dr. King, Malcolm X, and Medgar Evers blur together as the shadowy victims of an alien era of violence. Part of the reason for this ignorance is that over the last decade or so the aspirations of a striking number of black adolescents have shifted away from political goals defined in the 1960s, have shifted away even from the yearning for full status in the middle class that is still cover-story material in American magazines. Thanks mostly to shrewd packaging and enormous investments by white entrepreneurs, a large proportion of black teenage boys have adopted for their idols not the evangelists of equality but the towering black superstars of professional sports. Dr. J is a more compelling role model than Dr. King. It is not exaggerating much to say that the black boys at Bingham yearned not for equality in America but for supremacy and transcendence on the courts of the NBA.

The quest for superstardom has changed high school basketball dramatically. The tantalizing TV images of the pros have turned the boys against each other. They don't play like teammates; they play like superstars. Each one has a distinctive style: Robert Duncan has the deadly moves; on the free-throw line he bounces the ball once with his right hand, once with his left, once again with his right, once again with his left, and then shoots, feet far apart, almost without looking at the basket. John Brainerd can dribble between his legs with either hand; his favorite shot is a tricky lay-up in which he jumps into the air, spins away from the basket, and hammers the ball in off the boards on his way back around. "Hinkley" Jones shoots flat-footed, propelling the ball straight at the basket with an almost delicate snap of the wrists; after he shoots he lets his wrists go limp and takes two little half-steps backward with his toes pointed together. The important thing is not so much whether you make the basket, but whether you have any *style*.

One day after gym Les Zulinski and I watched Hinkley dribble the length of the empty court for a lay-up, and then come in again, in slow motion, from the free-throw line—his own instant replay. Another day in gym, when rain kept us indoors, away from soccer and field hockey, the black boys in the class played an informal basketball game on one half of the court. To make for more shooting opportunities, they used three goals, the main one at the end and the practice goals on either side. The game was a frantic free-for-all with no real teams, only loose alliances that dissolved and reformed every time the ball changed hands.

One day some of the black kids were sitting in the bleachers in the gym, waiting for Mr. Meiden to let the class out for lunch.

"Hinkley went to basketball camp. It didn't do him no good."

"He can't shoot."

"He can jump, though."

"But he can't make a jump *shot*."

"I thought you was supposed to be so good because you practiced all summer."

"That was last summer."

"Shit."

"There ain't enough varsity uniforms for you guys. I already got mine."

"I don't need no uniform, 'cause I got the deadly moves."

"Four juniors started varsity last year."

"They got a sophomore this year that everybody's talking about."

"He could be good but he didn't never play till he was in the eighth grade. He don't have no *style*. He could play on JV but not on varsity. Big kid with glasses."

"He don't have glasses this year."

"Maybe he got contacts."

"He's about six five."

"We gonna have to rough him up."

"Or maybe he's six six."

"We definitely gonna have to rough him up."

"What about that Washington?"

"Washington needs some hands."

"He plays three sports. That's too much."

"Unless he change his mind after football, he won't go out for basketball probably."

"That's just fine with me."

"If I was a little taller I could dunk it."

"You couldn't dunk it if you was standing on the rim."

"Maybe if you was to spread a little cheese on the rim, that boy'd be able to do it."

"Cheese wouldn't do no good."

"Man, I could do it in my stockin' feet."

"Them Hogan boys last year thought they was in for a joke, laughing and fooling around, and then we almost beat 'em."

"That was the worst game we played all year."

"No it wasn't. Every game was worse than all the others."

"But we kept coming back. We only lost to Prep by two points."

"Those mothers were *big*."

"Big and white."

"They got the *biggest* boys."

"We scrimmaged them and lost by seven."

"Ain't they supposed to have a real big freshman?"

"Yeah, he's big. In the head. He already got the biggest head I ever saw. Wants everybody to kiss his ass. He's left-handed. He won't be a threat till he's a sophomore."

"You jump off your right foot if you left-handed."

"*You* can't even make a lay-up."

"That was last year."

"You won't even make the team."

"Shit."

"He'll make it. They gonna need somebody to cool down the ball after I get through makin' my deadly moves."

The basketball team isn't the only student organization whose racial composition has changed over the last decade. The Library Club, an all-white girls' service organization throughout the sixties, is now about half black. A similar transformation has taken place in the Office Corps, which by 1979 had only two white members. Most of the major organizations, though, either have remained almost entirely white or have returned to that state after a brief period of integration early in the seventies. Of the fifty-five members of the student council when I was at Bingham, only four were black.

The consistently sparse representation of blacks in Bingham's important student organizations resembles the awkward tokenism of a decade ago, but there are important differences. The class of 1980 would be very unlikely to elect a black president of the student council, which is something the class of 1969 did; but the class of 1980 might very well elect a black chairman of the Thanksgiving Canned-Food Drive, or send a black delegate to a local conference on first-aid techniques. When each homeroom was asked to nominate one boy and one girl for Winter Cotillion King and Queen, the members of my homeroom, who had little enthusiasm for the Cotillion, were unable to come up with any names. Mr. Amberson solved our problem by suggesting that we nominate Ernest Lewis and Betsy Mayfair, a black boy and black girl in our homeroom. Blacks at Bingham accumulated small, unwanted honors the way pieces of furniture gather dust.

Blacks and whites at Bingham live in wary tolerance of each other. There is no violence in the halls, there are no attempts by militant black students to organize their classmates, there are no armbands, no petitions, no lists of grievances or demands. Blacks and whites are polite to one another but suspicious, noncombative but aloof. They do not beat each other up or shout each other down. Still, the lack of friction is evidence less of conciliation than of stalemate. At lunchtime the black students eat in a private corner of the cafeteria that is exactly three tables wide by six tables long. Before school they gather in the same corners and doorways, both inside and outside the building. They have their own hangouts, their own activities, virtually their own curriculum: Although there are no courses in black studies or African history at Bingham, black students, especially the boys, tend to cluster in courses they have made their own: Vocational Foods, Practical Math, Modern Communication. It sometimes seems as though the blacks and whites are students at two different schools, schools that just happen to be, housed in a single building.

Overt racism is rare, but it does exist, chiefly in the form of graffiti on lavatory walls, where new slurs crop up as quickly as the janitorial staff can scrub them away:

I hate niggers

Me Too

K
K
K

I love white people

dont hate
love your enemy
John Paul II
LOVE

Black is great
and tan is grand
but white
is the color of
an American

unknown poet

Ku Klux Klan

Head Kleagle C. A.

Niggers Blow

Support your local KKK

Roses are red
Violets are blue
I hate niggers
So do you

Classic white liberal guilt is a scarce commodity in the town of Bingham. Local government is a small-time operation made up mostly of unsalaried caretakers and citizens' committees. Few of the positions are held by blacks. Although the proportion of blacks to whites in the Bingham population is higher than that in the general population, there is no sense of a strong, supportive black community. Black leaders in the area tend to focus their energies on the problems of a nearby urban center where racial tensions are high.

Most black families in Bingham live in neighborhoods some distance from the center of town. Although Bingham High has been able to achieve mandated racial balance without importing minority students from beyond the school district, virtually all of the black students (as well as a roughly equal number of white students) travel to and from school on buses. Bus service is provided free to all students who live more than two miles from school, and most of the blacks live at least that distance away. When school ends for the day, the students walking home along the main drag—carrying books or musical instruments and wearing letter jackets or senior hats—are white. The black students roll by in their big yellow buses and turn off at the center of town toward the two-mile line.

The yearbook collection at the Bingham Public Library gives

a glimpse into the evolving sociology of Bingham High School. Although at first glance the *Banner*s from the last fifteen years look like the work of a single hand—only the covers and the clothing styles seem to change—there are subtle differences. In the 1966 and 1967 yearbooks, blacks are almost entirely absent from the candid photographs scattered among the set shots. The black presence at Bingham was smaller then than it is today, but even that fact is not sufficient to account for the uniform whiteness of the faces. In one of the few photographs in which blacks appear, a picture of an audience in the auditorium, two black girls—the only blacks in the picture—are isolated from their classmates by a buffer of empty seats.

By 1969 black students begin to appear more prominently. In a sprawling collage covering two pages at the beginning of the book, three of the pictures are of black students. Further on are shots of black students in a history class, a black boy in the library reading *The Battle of El Alamein,* a black girl cooking something in a home economics class, a black football player on crutches, two black women in a classroom on Parents' Night, a black couple at the senior prom. (Notably, the student council's president is that organization's only black member.) The trend continues through the early seventies. Black faces are sprinkled throughout the book, and more black students appear as members of school organizations. Especially conspicuous are the increasing numbers of black students pictured at dances.

And then, in the second half of the 1970s, the black faces begin to disappear again. In the *Banner* of 1979, a year in which the school's black population was about 250, there are hardly half a dozen candid photographs that show any blacks whatsoever. In the course of slightly more than a decade, in the pages of a dozen high school yearbooks, it is possible to witness the death and the rebirth of the Invisible Man.

On page 67 of the 1979 Bingham High School *Banner* is a photograph of the Junior Class Council. There are about thirty-five kids in the picture, arranged in three rows on risers on the stage in the auditorium. All the kids in the first two rows are white. Two of the kids in the last row, Rupert Landry and Howard Bennett, are black. Rupert is fourth from the left, Howard is fourth from the right. If you were to cut the picture vertically down the middle and lay one half on top of the other so that the images were touching, Rupert and Howard would be looking each other directly in the eye. The arrangement of black and white faces in the photograph is perfectly symmetrical.

On page 81 of the 1979 *Banner* is a photograph of the Ushers' Guild. One of the ushers, Joyce Daley, is black. She is standing precisely in the center of the last row.

On page 100 of the 1979 *Banner* is a photograph of the French Honor Society. Precisely in the center of the back row is Louis Clinton, the only black student in the picture.

On page 110 of the 1979 *Banner* is a photograph of the cheerleaders. The two black cheerleaders, Carol Jones and Mary Spanner, are at either end of the third row, the farthest to the left and the farthest to the right.

On page 121 of the 1979 *Banner* is a photograph of the soccer team. There are two black students in the picture, Ernest Jones and John Tucker. Ernest is sitting at the extreme left end of the second row, John at the extreme right.

On page 123 of the 1979 *Banner* is a photograph of the cross-country team. Kurt Ferrell, the only black student on the team, is standing precisely in the center of the back row.

On page 124 of the 1979 *Banner* is a photograph of the girls' basketball team. There are three black girls in the picture, Cynthia Wynn, Carol Jones, and Pamela Lewis. All three are sitting together, in the middle of the second row, with one white girl to the right and one white girl to the left.

On page 132 of the 1979 *Banner* is a photograph of the girls' softball team. There is one black student, Joyce Daley, in the picture. She is standing precisely in the center of the last row.

19
∾Grades

If you don't like trouble, don't eat meals with grown-ups.

"Isn't it about time for a haircut?" Ann asked.

"I'm letting it grow for the duration," I said.

"It's getting pretty long."

"It's part of my disguise."

"None of the other kids in your class have hair that long."

"How would you know?"

"I saw them at the dance."

"Some of them do," I said feebly.

"It's still too long."

Ann was right, as usual. I hadn't had my hair cut since the middle of the summer, and by now, November, I was looking shaggy. There *were* plenty of kids in my class whose hair was longer than mine, but most of them were hoods. Long hair isn't standard equipment for boys anymore at Bingham High. I'm not sure why I hadn't noticed that. It may be simply that I had reverted to my old high school self of a decade before. Long hair then made what seemed like a clear statement. But whatever it meant then, it didn't mean the same thing now. So, after a week of foot-dragging, I got a haircut. And the week after that, I got my grades.

George Menaro opened his denim jacket to show me the pieces of paper he had taped inside it. There was one on either side, fastened to the lining with masking tape. Each was covered with tiny handwriting in blue ballpoint.

"We got a physics test today," George said, "and I've got practically the whole fucking chapter written in my jacket."

He untucked his black Led Zeppelin T-shirt and rolled it carefully up over his stomach. There were two more pieces of paper taped inside it.

"The teacher knows where to look for them in my jacket," he explained, "so that's why I did it under my shirt, too. He'll look inside the jacket and say, 'Aha', and make me take it off, but I'll still have the stuff inside my shirt."

"I'm just gonna leave my book open," George's friend Andy said.

"How are you going to lift your shirt up like that during the test without the teacher seeing you?" I asked George.

"Look, man," he said, rolling up his shirt again. "I've got the paper in there *upside down,* so I can read it just by looking down at it. All I gotta do is slouch down and pull up my shirt."

"But then if he catches you," Andy said, "you ain't exactly gonna be able to say you didn't know what you was doing."

"Yeah," George said, "I'll just say my mom accidentally wrote all the answers in my clothes while she was doing the laundry."

"If he sees you with your book open," Andy said, "all you gotta do is say you forgot to close it."

"Yeah," George said, "like you just happened to turn it to the page that all the questions were about, and then you just happened to leave it open."

"Big deal," Andy said. "That guy'd believe anything you told him."

"He thinks he's such a smart ass," George said. "He's always telling these big jokes."

"He can't control the class worth a shit."

"We just fuck around and ruin all the equipment. They never have any good stuff, anyway."

"Over at Eisenhower," Andy said, "I knew this kid in chemistry, and they had all this fucking acid that would burn right through the fucking table, man."

"I burned up my transformer," George said.

"How much did you have to pay?"

"I didn't have to pay nothin', because I did it by accident. But Larry Dimeno used to burn 'em up on purpose, just to see 'em smoke."

Cheating is a fact of life in a high school, especially as report-card time draws near. Bingham's first marking period ended early in November, and in the last days before the deadline, students with marginal averages went all out. A couple of weeks before, "warning notes" had been mailed to the parents of kids who were in danger of flunking, and now the push was on. In history particularly, where opportunities were plentiful, the cheating was intense.

The champion cribber in history was Arnold Jensen, who sat a few desks away from mine. He was very conspicuous about it. He kept his notebook open in his lap during tests, consulted his textbook when he couldn't find the answer in his notes, and asked the kids sitting near him for answers in a loud whisper even when Mr. Bartlett was in the room. When Mr. Bartlett went down the hall for a few minutes, Arnold would sometimes get up out of his chair and walk across the room to consult with other kids. A lot of the kids were reluctant to take part in such blatant rule-breaking—although most of them cheated in smaller ways—but there is a code of honor in a high school that prevents all but the most sanctimonious students from objecting too forcefully. Most of the kids at least let Arnold look over their shoulders—and so did I—although more than a few refused to let him actually pick up their test papers so he could examine them more closely. Arnold's compulsion to cheat was so over-powering that he did it even when he knew the answers; he didn't feel comfortable until he had confirmed everything with independent sources.

Like a lot of inveterate cheaters, Arnold was a real stickler for accuracy as far as other people were concerned. After quizzes, Mr. Bartlett usually had us trade papers and grade them as he read off the answers. Arnold would raise his hand repeatedly as we went over the quizzes, trying to find technicalities for which he could penalize the person whose paper he was grading. Once, when he was grading my paper, he read one of my answers aloud and asked Mr. Bartlett whether he should count it completely wrong or give me partial credit. "No, Arnold," Mr. Bartlett said, "that's just the right answer." Arnold reluctantly scratched out his check mark and began to pick apart my next answer.

The final week or two before report-card day was hectic for the teachers. Many of the ones who hadn't finished marking papers or averaging grades took time off to catch up on paperwork. For the two days before report cards came out, Mr. Potter, in math, and Mr. Chapin, in psychology, were the only teachers of mine who showed up at school (one of those days, Mr. Chapin spent the entire period reading Polish jokes aloud from a paperback book); all my other classes were taught by substi-tutes. "Report card flu," Mr. Potter called it. He, of course, was immune.

Those two days at the end of the grading period were two of the longest I spent at Bingham. There just wasn't anything to do. As usual, most of the boys gazed silently into space and waited for the minutes to tick away. I was constantly amazed at how long my schoolmates could sit and do absolutely nothing at all; television-watching may be good training in that regard. About a quarter of the kids in my first-period study hall didn't even bring their school books into the room; they just crossed their arms and looked at the clock or, if they were facing the other direction, the wall. On those two days when most of my classes were taught by substitutes, I kept a novel in my notebook, but I never dared to open it; *reading* would have been about as inconspicuous as building a fire in my desk.

In journalism, though, no one sat and stared. Bill managed to persuade our substitute that Mrs. Griswold ordinarily encouraged us to spend class time selling ads to local businesses. The substitute said, "Well, if that's what you're supposed to do . . ." So half a dozen of us stuffed advertising contracts into our pockets and took off to laze around in the parking lot of a nearby shopping center. Just before we returned, we filled out a few of the contracts with the names of businesses in the shopping center and handed them in when we returned.

Mr. Chapin averted a last-minute crunch for himself by having us figure out our own grades. He read our scores aloud and let us do the averaging. One of the girls saw this as a good opportunity to add a dozen points to her average, but it turned out that Mr. Chapin had already done all the figuring himself and was merely using us to check his arithmetic.

"Take me for a dummy, eh?" Mr. Chapin said.

"It was worth a try," the girl muttered.

"Aw, come on," Mr. Chapin said, "even if I *hadn't* averaged them already, there's no way in the world a fifty-two, a forty-five, a sixty-one, and a sixty-four could work out to a seventy."

"Then why'd ya ask me, huh? You was just trying to tempt us."

As the rest of us read off our scores, it became obvious that something like a quarter of the kids in the class were going to flunk. Someone suggested that we be allowed to throw out the lowest of our five test scores, and after a little argument, Mr.

Chapin consented. But even this wasn't enough to save everybody.

"Let us take off another, huh, Mr. Chapin?" said the girl who had earlier tried to add points to her score.

"I'd love to, sweetheart, but even if I let you get rid of all but *one* of them you still wouldn't pass."

Bingham's record-keeping system is not computerized, so all transcripts and report cards have to be filled out by hand. On report-card day we were all issued the necessary forms in homeroom and told to carry them from class to class the rest of the day. Once again, most of my teachers took the day off and let the substitutes handle the paperwork. This led to some confusion. In English, Mr. Quennell's substitute, an immense, slovenly man named Mr. LaFleur, momentarily got his papers shuffled and began to give us the grades from another section. There was a brief silence. The kids were trying to figure out whether this would work out to some kind of advantage. But then Mr. LaFleur caught his error.

After he had given us our grades, Mr. LaFleur quizzed us on our vocabulary. One of the words on the list was *radiation,* and the sentence given to illustrate its meaning was, "The experts were worried that the world might be destroyed by *radiation* from a nuclear war."

"Now here," Mr. LaFleur said, "is an example of the author inserting his own opinions into his writings. They do the same thing on television programs. Now, I have been a student of civil defense for many years. In the event of nuclear war, all life would not be destroyed. To the unsophisticating person, nuclear war seems like a very terrible thing. But a percentage would be left. If you believe the world is going to end, you'll do anything to keep it from ending, and this leads to all kinds of problems. The thing is that radiation would result in more children born deformed. What we have to remember is that children are even now born deformed. A very small percent. In a war, of course, this would be higher, but it would still be a percent."

My grades were pretty good, although the order they fell in surprised me. My lowest marks were in English and history, 80 and 81 respectively. I got an 84 in psychology. In math I got a 91, which turned out to be the highest grade, and the only A, in the class. I felt guilty about that, but also pleased: I am not accustomed to making A's in math courses. My best grade was in accounting, where I got a 95—but all the scores were high in accounting. My 95 may not even have put me in the top quarter of the class.

At the end of the day a special homeroom period was declared so we could turn in our transcript cards. When I got to homeroom, Mr. Amberson's seventh-period English class (all seniors) was just letting out. Their vocabulary list was still on the blackboard:

1. buy	8. then	15. all ready
2. to	9. their	16. way
3. they're	10. too	17. rather
4. weak	11. than	18. truly
5. by	12. week	19. quit
6. there	13. weigh	20. whether
7. two	14. always	

Mr. Amberson's class was studying Shakespeare at the moment. He said they had been "going over" *Hamlet,* because "it takes too long to read it, really." So they had been discussing the "plot" all period.

After we handed in our transcript cards, Mr. Amberson told us we could go, even though there were still a few minutes left in the school day. Just as I was leaving, the assistant principal announced over the public address system that students must remain in their homerooms until the official closing time, 2:15.

"Homeroom teachers," the voice said, "are hereby instructed to make a list of anyone not present and send it down to the office immediately." Mr. Amberson quickly made a list of the students he had just excused. "Where the heck are those guys?" he muttered.

At home that night I dutifully called Julia to report my grades.

"I got two A's and three B's," I said.

"What!!?" she screamed. "How did you get three D's?"

"*B's,*" I repeated. "Not D's."

"Oh," she said. She paused. "But you could still do better."

20
Eisenhower-10, Bingham-0

Be it resolved, that the first touchdown scored by Bingham High School in Saturday's game with Eisenhower will be dedicated to the Class of 1980.

By proclamation of the
student council, Nov. 14, 1979

The last time Bingham High School won the Inter-Valley Conference Championship in football was 1969. That was the year that George Meyer, Arnie Falkowskie, Todd D'Angelo, and Joe Henley were on the team. All four were linemen who played both offense and defense, and together they weighed about as much as the rest of the squad combined. They were four tough mothers. In one game, Falkowskie, who on defense played nose guard, blitzed through the line at warp speed, took the handoff from the astonished opposing quarterback, and carried it forty-five yards for a touchdown. After that the coach wanted to move him to fullback, but Arnie wouldn't budge. He said there wasn't enough glory in the backfield; all the *real* nut-crunching took place on the line.

There were giants in the earth in those days. More recently —in the closing months of this year, for instance—the Bingham Bombers had not been so imposing. Although by the middle of November the boys had scrambled their way to an even record, their victories had had as much to do with mistakes made by their opponents as with anything they themselves had done. Even some of the guys on the team were saying that they weren't playing any better now than they had been during the first week of September. And that was the week when a fired-up team from a neighboring town had embarrassed them 54–0.

To make matters worse, the only game now remaining in the season, the November 17 match with crosstown nemesis Eisenhower High, was almost certain to be a stinker. The Generals had dropped only one game all fall and were considered by some to be the best team in the state. If Bingham meant to carry the day and salvage a winning record for the year, it was going to have to put in a performance worthy of a Rose Bowl contender. Either that or hope for a sudden outbreak of polio in the Eisenhower locker room.

Or so said Les Zulinski. Les and I were sitting in the cafeteria after gym, discussing football strategy. I was telling him about a garbage play called Screwball: On first down the offensive team forms its huddle on the line of scrimmage, about fifteen yards from the ball. The linemen, in the huddle, put their heels on the line of scrimmage and get set. The center wanders over to the ball and shouts, "Hey, you idiots, the ball's over here!" He then swoops it off the ground and spins it over to the quarterback, who trots it into the end zone before the defense can figure out what's going on. A guaranteed six points, and perfectly legal. All you have to do is tell the ref about it beforehand. My old ninth-grade team used it in one game and the varsity was so impressed they picked it up for themselves.

"I may have heard of that before," Les said, "but I don't know, Dave. It's not exactly my style."

"Oh, well," I said. "It sounded like you guys could use some help."

And indeed it did. The tables nearest ours were fairly buzzing with talk about the game, little of it optimistic. Principal Shenck—possibly believing that his own honor was as much at stake as the team's—had called a giant pep rally for the next day, the Friday before the game. It would be the first pep rally since a chaotic assembly back in September when the cheerleaders, the Bomberettes, and the members of all the boys' and girls' teams had been introduced. On that inauspicious occasion, the "Star-Spangled Banner" soloist, singing into a microphone at one end of the gym, and the school band, playing too quietly at the other, had gotten so hopelessly out of sync with each other that the soloist had had to hum for a couple of beats to let the musicians catch up. But this time it was going to be different. The game with Eisenhower was genuinely important, and the band had had two and a half months to get its act together.

The bell rang at 1:20 on Friday, with ten minutes still to go in sixth period, and all classes emptied into the halls. I ran into Bill and Eric over by the Publications Office and walked to the gym with them. When we got there the band was grinding through a song I eventually recognized as the *Pink Panther* theme. "They're every bit as good as they used to be," Bill said. The cheerleaders were arranging themselves on the basketball court. Sheila McNichols was under the far goal. She suddenly dropped into the splits, looking for a moment as though a trapdoor had opened beneath her. "How the hell do they do that, man?" Eric said. "I bet they'll all get cancer of the pussy from landing on the floor like that." The other cheerleaders were practicing swishing sidesteps, or pulling loose streamers from their pompoms, or just sitting cross-legged on the floor.

Bill, Eric, and I found seats up near the top of the senior section of the bleachers. After the national anthem had been played and sung in unison, the president of the student athletic association stepped up to the microphone under the scoreboard.

"With great personal pleasure," he said, "I would like to introduce you to your Bingham High School cheerleaders for this year and their cocaptains, Jennifer Amanso and Cynthia Jordan." Jennifer and Cynthia were both in journalism. Bill, Eric, and I clapped. The band struck up the *Star Wars* theme and the fourteen cheerleaders began to dance a sort of sanitized Bugaloo. They were spaced evenly around the perimeter of the half-court nearer the microphone, five on either side and four across the center line. When the music stopped the cocaptains stepped into the middle and shouted, "Hello Cheer! Ready? Okay!" and began to sound off:

"I'm Jenny!" Stomp-stomp stomp-stomp-stomp stomp-stomp-stomp-stomp STOMP STOMP.

"I'm Cindy!" Stomp-stomp stomp-stomp-stomp stomp-stomp-stomp-stomp STOMP STOMP.

In the middle of this cheer a fat boy with shoulder-length hair sitting a few rows down from us shouted, "Cheerleaders make better lovers!" and got a big laugh. We were all supposed to be making noise, but not many of the people sitting near us were. Most of the school spirit in our section was confined to the front few rows, where virtually all of the kids (most of them girls) were wearing senior hats. There were a few frustrated enthusiasts up near us, however. One of them, Mark Carpenter, a boy in my gym class, kept turning to people sitting behind him and saying, "Hey! Let's get rowdy!" or "Come on now, let's get *really* rowdy!" or "All right! Now let's really get *rowdy* this time!" In gym Mark was famous for his imitations of *Monty Python* and *Saturday Night Live* routines. He was always tugging nervously at other people's T-shirts and saying things like, "Hey, man, did you see the twit routine on *Python*? Huh? Huh?" During the Victory Cheer ("V-I-C-T-O-R-Y, that's the Bingham Battle Cry!") the fat kid with the long hair shouted "R-O-L-A-I-D-S!")

Virtually everyone, boy and girl, was keeping a close watch on the cheerleaders. Even back in my day, when all the girls wore short skirts, a cheerleader's legs were something to be reckoned with. Nowadays, when hemlines have crept back closer to the floor, the sight of twenty-eight long bare brown legs kicking and sliding in unison right there in the good old gym can be close to overwhelming. Earlier in the day, Lou Murphy, the black class comedian, had shaken his head and said to one of his teachers, "The cheerleaders' skirts just get shorter and shorter." Now someone was shouting, "Do the can-can!" repeatedly, to no avail. When, at the end of one cheer, the girls pivoted away from the bleachers, bent forward, and flipped the backs of their skirts up into the air, a little astonished gasp flashed through the crowd.

After a dozen cheers the girls lined up on either side of the free-throw lane and raised their pompoms over their heads. The locker room doors burst open and the football team, in game uniforms but without helmets, shoes, or shoulder pads, emerged. They jogged between the two rows of cheerleaders and spread out on the center line. I spotted Les in the middle of the pack. The cheerleaders jumped and shook their pompoms. The brass section of the band sounded a cavalry charge.

The crowd cheered with some enthusiasm. Coach Meiden, wearing a bright purple sport coat and carrying a clipboard, stepped up to the microphone.

"Before I say anything at all," he said, "I just want to thank this year's fabulous cheerleaders. Aren't they terrific. Girls, you're gorgeous. And I want to mention one thing: These girls have so much spirit and so much enthusiasm that they paid their own money out of their own pockets to buy their numerals and name patches. Isn't that something?" Coach Meiden made a chivalrous little nod in the direction of the free-throw lane and some of the boys whistled.

Bill caught Amy's eye. She was sitting two sections over with a bunch of girls. He waved to her, then thumbed his nose affectionately. Eric, meanwhile, was giving him the old donkey ears.

"Now a word about Eisenhower," Mr. Meiden said, "who, as you know, is our opponent tomorrow. It's a tough team, I'll admit it. They were state champions two years ago. They've got eighty boys on the squad and a coaching staff of ten. They've got a brand-new practice field. They've got new equipment. And they've got a couple of stars. But even though they've only been beaten once this year, I'm not pessimistic. I would remind you that school spirit can make the difference between victory and defeat. So get out there tomorrow and make it happen!"

The band played "Hail, Bingham!" and everyone stood. The kids in the first few rows locked arms and swayed back and forth as they sang. The cheerleaders formed a circle in their end of the court and waved their pompoms slowly over their heads. "Give me the fucking creeps," Bill said. When the music stopped, Principal Shenck took the microphone:

"I have several things I'd like to say, but before I do, there are a few comments I'd like to direct to the seniors." He pulled a senior hat out of his jacket pocket and put it on his head. The seniors went wild. "If you remember," he continued, "when I announced this pep assembly yesterday, I urged each and every one of you to wear your school colors to this rally today. But I see that only a few of you actually did. You few, I salute. But tomorrow I want to see all of you in purple and gold. Let's show Eisenhower we really know what we're up to!"

Most of the kids jumped to their feet and shouted and stomped on the bleachers. The noise was terrific. Bill put his hands over his ears and moaned theatrically. The cheerleaders were a frenzy of arms and legs. The principal motioned for silence.

"And now, before the cheerleaders lead us in a final cheer, I would like to remind you to please, after the assembly is over, exit the gymnasium in a mature and orderly manner."

Burlington Field, where both Bingham and Eisenhower play their home games, is a semipublic football field in the middle of Town Park, about halfway between the two schools. The Bingham school system pays an annual rental fee to the town and turns the proceeds from ticket sales, less a certain percentage, back to the athletic departments of the individual schools. I made my way over about twenty minutes early and saw one of the cheerleaders walking in the same direction. She was wearing sneakers and carrying her saddle shoes in one hand and her pompoms in the other. At the gate I paid three dollars for my ticket and went inside.

The stands were still mostly empty. Some of the band members were warming up, and Ricky Roberts, pride of the audiovisual department, was assembling videotape equipment on top of the press box. I saw Carl Morgan, the photo editor of the *Bomber,* standing on the sidelines with his camera, and went over to say hello.

"Hey, Dave," he said. "What are you doing here?"

"I figured I ought to come see what the team looks like."

"You'll see, all right. You pay to get in?"

"Yep. Three bucks."

"You got stiffed. You shoulda showed 'em your press pass. I just went up and pointed to the camera and said, 'School photographer,' and the guy let me in for nothin'."

Both teams were on the field now, doing warm-up calisthenics. The Eisenhower kids were doing the basics—leg-lifts, sit-ups, jumping jacks—while the Bombers ran through an exotic repertoire of isometric exercises, most of which involved two or three participants and half a dozen balletlike posturings of arms, legs, and torsos. When all were sufficiently limber, the boys on both teams paired off for shoulder- and helmet-popping, then formed squads for passing and blocking drills.

I decided it was time to find a seat. Bingham had been declared home team for the day, so we had the better bleachers. I climbed to the top row and sat near the press box. Other than the cheerleaders and the kids in the band, there were only about a dozen students present, few of whom I recognized. By far the largest contingent was a noisy group of parents and alumni sitting together off to the left. They had blankets and seat cushions and Thermoses and beer. The cheerleaders were milling around in front of the bleachers with a couple of solicitous mothers in attendance. The mothers were circulating hairbrushes and holding up hand mirrors so the girls could check their makeup.

By 1:30 the crowd had grown to a more respectable size, although there was still a shortage of students. If Principal Shenck was present, I did not see him, but Mr. Bartlett, along with his wife and two children, was sitting in the front row. Linda Smoley was in the press box, barking orders to a trio of languid sophomores. A little thunder rumbled in the distance. As the captains of both teams walked to the center of the field for the coin toss, the first few drops of rain began to fall.

Bingham won the toss. The band played the national anthem. And the football game began. Bomber running back Luke D'Amato took the kickoff on about the thirty, changed direction twice, and got as far as his own forty. In three plays the Bomber offense moved the ball backward to the twenty-five. Mike Gibson, the punter, booted it back up to about the forty. The Eisenhower Generals, in two quick fullback smashes, marched the ball to the five, then fumbled. The Bombers advanced five yards in three plays, and Mike Gibson punted out of bounds at the thirty-five. The Generals chewed up fifteen yards with an end sweep and then threw a perfect pass to a startled Bomber defenseman. Les Zulinski threw three incompletions, and Mike Gibson punted out of bounds at the thirty-five.

And so on, for the entire first quarter. The Bombers never left their end of the field, and the Generals never set foot in theirs. Still, the Generals did not score. There were two time-outs, three fumbles, and no completed passes, except for two interceptions. The sun peeked out briefly at one point, then disappeared for good. The band played through it all: "Light My Fire," "25 or 6 to 4," "Fever," "Get It On." At the end of "Get It On," a saxophonist sitting near the press box turned to a fellow musician and said, "Geez, I still had two measures to go."

A light rain fell intermittently, but it was so gentle few people bothered to open umbrellas. On the field, though, where there was already more mud than grass, things began to get a little sloppy. Blockers slipped, running backs stumbled, and both quarterbacks had trouble keeping their hands on the ball. Conditions were almost as bad in front of the bleachers, where the cheerleaders were going through their paces. Over the course of the season, the girls had pounded the grass behind the team bench into extinction. Now there was nothing there but a shallow basin of mud. As the afternoon wore on, the girls had to pause frequently to scrape the soles of their saddle shoes or wipe splatters from their legs. Several of their cheers required the smaller girls to climb onto the shoulders or backs of the others, and when they did they left brown footprints on white sweaters.

People who know about such things distinguish two major cheerleading styles, stomp (or dance) and precision. Stomp cheerleading is loose and bouncy, with lots of hip-swinging, foot-pounding, and rhythmic hand-clapping. It is designed to take advantage of the hardwood floor and washtub acoustics of a high school gymnasium. Precision cheerleading, on the other hand, is a mostly visual style. It is intended primarily for football stadiums, where sounds don't carry as well as they do indoors. A precision cheerleader moves her arms and legs with a robotlike severity and uses a crisp, exaggerated diction. Her arm motions look like military salutes. Most of the fancy acrobatics in cheerleading are associated with the stomp method rather than the precision method, if only because it is easier (and safer) to do the splits on a basketball court than on a cinder track.

Or in a sea of mud. Bingham's cheerleaders are classic stompers. They wear hard-soled saddle shoes instead of Keds, and nearly every one of their cheers is punctuated with vigorous hand-clapping and soulful stomping. At the pep assembly on Friday the girls sounded great, kicking up a clatter that rang through the gym, but at the football game they sounded a little thin. Every time they stomped their feet, their shoes sucked silently into the muck. It must have been disheartening for them, but still they persevered. At one point Sheila McNichols and another girl even attempted a double cartwheel ending in the splits, and got more than they bargained for when they landed.

With only a couple of minutes remaining in the half, the inevitable finally happened. The Eisenhower quarterback, with time to spare, closed his eyes at the center of the field and heaved a perfect, arcing forty-yard spiral directly to his receiver standing all alone on the Bomber ten. There wasn't a purple shirt in sight. The receiver strolled into the end zone and the score was six to nothing. Bingham's fans began to mutter, but the cheerleaders leaped into the breach:

> Look Cheer! Ready? Okay!
> Hey, look us over,
> Pride of B.H.S.
> Tops in the area, always give our best
> Band is smart-appearing.
> Team among the best.
> And when it comes to faculty,
> We'll take ours above the rest.

And we'll always be there fighting,
Spirit way up high.
Cheerleaders yelling; come on, kids, let's jive.
We're the top pride of our community,
High hopes all rest with us.
So come on, team,
BOUNCE!

On the conversion attempt, the Eisenhower center flubbed his snap. The kicker scooped up the bouncing ball and ran it wide for two. The following kick-off was delayed while the manual scoreboard keeper, a bedraggled sophomore named Howdie Bascom, sifted through his pile of numerals for an eight. There is no clock at Burlington Field, so time-keeping is a mystery concealed from the fans. Almost before the Bombers could mount their first play, the second quarter ended without fanfare. Both teams retired to a small stone field house outside the gates, and the cheerleaders bolted for the concession stand.

I scanned the sidelines for Carl Morgan but didn't see him. Apparently he had snapped a few shots and departed. Just as I was about to go buy a Coke, Bill and Amy appeared around the corner of the press box.

"Dave baby."

"I didn't know you guys were here."

"We just got here. How's the game?"

"Sucks."

"Just what I expected," Bill said. "But if you come late you don't have to pay."

They sat down beside me and Bill offered me half a hotdog.

"I only come for the halftime show," he said. "It's better than 'Mr. Bill.' Hey, Dave, Eddie Lober is having a big party in a couple of weeks. His parents are taking off for the Bahamas. You wanna go?"

"Sure. I've never been to the Bahamas."

"No, idiot, the party."

When the cheerleaders had all drifted back to the bleachers with Cokes and long strands of cherry licorice, the halftime entertainment began. The band played what their music sheets identified as "Football Fight Medley," a pastiche of Sousa marches and college songs. Then it was the cheerleaders' turn. They lined up along the sideline in front of the bench while their counterparts on the Eisenhower side did the same. Then both squads walked in step to the center of the field and fell into formation facing each other. The Bingham girls performed an elaborate greeting cheer that ended in a human pyramid. The Eisenhower girls reciprocated with a precision-style display. All the girls then formed a huge circle, locked arms, and bowed their heads. In this strange arrangement they remained for some time; then they broke up and ran back to their benches.

The band worked its way through another chunk of the "Fight Medley" while the Bomberettes took the field. The Bomberettes are essentially second-string cheerleaders, although they do not—let no one doubt it—lead cheers. Their domain is precision marching, banner-bearing, and coordinated dancing. Period. Their uniforms resemble the cheerleaders' uniforms, but instead of pleated gold skirts and billowy white sweaters, the Bomberettes wear straight-cut gold jumpers and long-sleeved, butterfly-collared Oxford-cloth shirts. Their pompoms have plastic straps instead of wooden handles. Neither their jumpers nor their shirts are decorated with name patches, numerals, or Bingham insignia. Their shoe laces are one color only. They have no megaphones. And yet, in spite of these handicaps, they manage to march right onto the field during halftime and do their act in front of everyone, even as the cheerleaders loll in the bleachers, deflecting the attentions of nonvarsity males and looking after their hairdos. It's got to take some nerve.

Even so, sad to say, the Bomberettes are boring. Part of the fault for this lies with the band, which accompanies all Bomberette routines. Another factor is the size of the squad: There are exactly the same number of Bomberettes as cheerleaders, and while fourteen can sometimes seem like an awful lot of cheer-leaders, it never quite seems like enough Bomberettes. They look lost out there, marching through the mud. And when they form their tiny, crooked kick-line for "Take It All Off," the effect is not what they surely have in mind.

"Well," Bill said, "I don't know how much of this I can take."

"You ought to stay for some of the game," I said.

"I don't know. Why don't you come and do something with us?"

"Yeah," Amy said.

This was tempting, but I was determined to watch the entire game. "I've got too much money invested in this," I said. "And anyway, I've got to meet my dad afterwards and do some stuff with him."

"That's tough," Bill said. "But you'll come to the party?"

"Sure. That'll be great."

"We might go to a movie first," Amy said.

"Maybe," Bill said.

"Hey, who's the one with the car?" Amy said.

"Okay, forget it. We can figure it out later. See ya around, Dave."

"Sure," I said. "See you on Monday."

Just before the second half began, Linda Smoley stuck her head out of the press box and asked if I would help her spot. Her sophomores had deserted her to run around under the bleachers smoking cigarettes, looking up skirts, and hunting for dropped wallets. I said sure and joined her in the press box. She handed me a mimeographed listing of the names and numbers of the players on both teams.

"Each time they run a play," she said, "you look on there and tell me who had the ball and who made the tackle, and I'll announce it." There was a microphone on the table in front of her. She turned it on and spoke. "Let's have a big round of applause for the band, everybody." She clicked it off and called down to one of her friends.

"Hey, Kimmy, you got any cigs?"

"Sorry."

"Dave?"

"Nope."

"Shit! Hey, Kimmy, go ask Sheila for some of her cigarettes."

"For*get* it."

"Bitch."

The two teams lined up for the kickoff and the referee blew his whistle. Linda turned on the microphone:

"Ladies and gentlemen, here comes the kickoff. We are beginning the third period of this football game here today. Bingham is kicking and Eisenhower is catching. Here comes the kick—and there's the kick." To me: "Dave, who's got it? Quick! Who's got the ball?"

I looked at my program. Maddeningly, the players were listed in alphabetical and not numerical order, so I had to scan the entire column of numbers to determine that number 22, the boy with the ball, was someone named John McGee. I told Linda.

"Who tackled him? Come on, Dave. And what yard were they on?"

"I have no idea."

"Oh, fuck!"

"Fake it," I said.

"What?"

"Just say he was brought down 'by various members of the other team.' "

"Fuck you."

On the next play I managed to identify all the principals, but still not fast enough to satisfy Linda.

"Here," I said, tearing the program down the middle. "Why don't you spot the Bingham guys and I'll look after Eisenhower?"

"But I'm the *announcer*."

"You can announce and still look at the program. You don't announce with your eyes."

"Goddammit!"

She consented, but her heart wasn't in it. She kept forgetting to look at the numbers of the players she was watching and expecting me to supply the information. I was having enough trouble keeping track of my own people. Eventually I realized she didn't care what she announced as long as she had something to say, so sometimes when I was in doubt I picked a name more or less at random. I was reminded a little sadly of the only time I ever did anything worthy of special mention in a football game: After snapping the ball on a punt during a junior varsity game in tenth grade, I ran down the field, tackled the receiver, knocked the ball from his hands, and scrambled on top of it. The voice from the press box blared: "Fumble recovered by Tim Regan." It broke my mother's heart.

Eisenhower ran a tricky reverse, and the player who ended up with the ball was someone new from the bench. He wasn't listed on my program.

"Who was that?" Linda screamed.

"I don't know. He isn't even on this thing."

She gave me a few more seconds, then shouted, "Who? Who?" and slapped me hard across the shoulders.

"Hey, fuck you," I said. I threw down the program. I was about to walk out on her when I noticed it was raining.

Fortunately, Linda apologized before I got wet. "Sorry, Dave," she said. "Didn't mean to get carried away." She picked up the program and held it out to me. I hesitated for a moment, then took it back. From then on we got along fine, if only because a few minutes later one of the errant sophomores returned and took over the home-team spotting.

The Bingham offense, meanwhile, was stuck on its own five-yard line. Les had tried two long passes without success. His passing method was to put the ball up high in the general vicinity of his receivers and their defenders, and let them sort things out for themselves. He was lucky that the other team was having as much trouble catching his passes as his own was. On third and long he faded back into the end zone for one last try.

Nobody was open. He tucked the ball under his arm and tried to make a dash for it. A linebacker caught him on his blind side and decked him between the goal posts. Safety. It was ten to nothing. Not even Screwball could have evened things up at that point.

Five minutes later the game was over. Both benches emptied onto the field and the players from the two teams grudgingly shook hands or patted one another on the back. Then the Generals, cheering, jogged off toward their team bus. The Bombers stayed put. A couple of them were crying, including Les Zulinski. The cheerleaders, a couple of whom were also crying, climbed onto the now-empty bench and looked out over the field. The few fans who were still in the stands stood behind them. The cheerleaders locked arms. Very quietly we began to sing "Hail, Bingham!"

Part Four

December

That is no country for old men. The young
In one another's arms . . .

—W. B. Yeats

21
∾ Par-tee

It used to be said, when I was in junior high and high school, that it was easier for a teenager to buy marijuana than beer. That may have been true then, but it certainly wasn't true when I was at Bingham. For most of the Bingham kids I knew, alcohol was the first and last word in getting high. Some, maybe even a lot, of the kids took drugs, but *all* of them got drunk, some more than others.

Greg Liszk, the boy I sat next to on the way to the Who concert in September, was far and away the champion beer hound in my circle of acquaintances at Bingham. Bill Scalet told me that Greg could chug a can of beer in five seconds, and "shoot" it in three seconds, and crush the empty on his forehead just like John Belushi in *Animal House*. Once he belched for thirty seconds straight, absolutely uninterrupted. He could put away a six-pack and then walk a straight line. Blindfolded. That's what everybody said. The only brand of beer he didn't like was Heineken. His favorite brand was Schlitz, "even though you have to pick the barley out of your teeth." He said beer out of a keg tasted like piss, but still, it was beer-piss. He also said, in study hall one morning, that he could drink a case of beer in thirty minutes. I wasn't there, but I heard about it later, at lunch. I was sitting at a table with Bill, Eric, Scott, and three or four other guys. Greg was at a table far across the cafeteria, letting his words soak in.

"How much will he back in bets?" Scott asked.

"I don't know. Couple hundred dollars."

"I can put up twenty."

"Shit, man, I'm bettin' fifty. It'll be the easiest money I ever made."

"How many ounces in a gallon?"

"How many gallons in a case?"

I multiplied some numbers on my napkin. "It's a little over two gallons," I said. "I don't think he could even drink that much *water* in a half hour."

"We're gonna fucking clean up."

"We gotta draw up a contract."

"We already did," one of the other guys said. "We did it second period. We get to pick the brand, anything except Heineken. If he does it, we pay for the beer and he keeps the bets. If he doesn't, he buys the beer and pays everybody off."

"We oughta get some of this St. Pauli Girl beer," Bill said. "It's like the heaviest beer there is."

"There's some kind of German beer my brother told me about that has something like fifteen percent alcohol."

"Let's get some of that. He'll be on his ass!"

"Find out the name from your brother."

"We can ask the guy at the liquor store what kind has the most alcohol," Bill said. "Tell him you like want to know because you're thinking of having a party and you want to buy the least amount of beer you can, you know, so he won't get suspicious."

I did some more calculations on my napkin. "In a case of regular beer," I said, "there's something like fourteen and a half ounces of pure alcohol. That's more than a whole can's worth of grain alcohol. There's no way he'd be able to drink it."

"We've got it made."

"We ought to put a drop of grain alcohol in the top of each can," Eric said. "He'll be on his ass inside fifteen minutes."

Greg came over to our table after lunch and said he'd been thinking it over and wanted to change a few of the rules. In the first place, he said, he wanted an hour instead of thirty minutes. A couple of the kids wanted to hold him to the original bet, but after a while someone said, "Let him *have* an hour, we'll still clean up." Next Greg said he wanted to be allowed to piss during the course of the hour. A couple of the kids started to worry about their money at that point, but finally someone said, "Let him *have* pissing." Then Greg said he wanted to be allowed to puke, too. Everybody screamed about that, but finally someone said, "Let him *have* puking," and that was that. All that remained to be done was to find a place where Greg could do it. And that place, it was finally decided, would be the party at Eddie Lober's.

Word had really gotten around about the party. Everybody, it seemed, was going, and Eddie was clearly enjoying the attention he was getting. He kept talking about what a rowdy time everybody was going to have. We were really going to par-*tee*. I didn't know Eddie very well, but I'd eaten lunch at the same table with him a couple of times. He was a small, stocky, nervous boy who was relentless in promoting his own popularity. He was a third- or fourth-string guard on the football team, but to hear him talk you'd have thought he was a star. At the Eisenhower game I watched him pace the sidelines with the coaches, his helmet strapped on and his mouthpiece in place, ready to storm the field on a moment's notice. But when the mudbath ended, his uniform was spotless: He hadn't played a minute. Even so, he was fiercely disdainful of anyone who wasn't on the team. If I hadn't been a friend of Les Zulinski's, I'm sure he wouldn't have bothered to talk to me at all. As it was, our single conversation was brief: "You ever play ball?" he asked me one day at lunch. "Just junior high and one year of JV," I said. And that was that.

Before the party, Bill and Amy and I, along with Scott, Eric, and Mary Humbert (the girl who had asked Bill to the Winter Cotillion), went to a movie. Because it was playing in another town, I couldn't arrange to meet the kids at the theater, as I had done when we went to see *Animal House*. I debated whether to let them pick me up at "home" but decided not to risk it. I said I had to run an errand for my father ("Dad" was a better provider of excuses than of money) and that it would be easier for me if I could be picked up at Bill's house, if that was okay with him. Fortunately, it was.

The movie we saw was *10,* a last-minute choice whose main attraction was the fact that none of us had seen it. When we left the theater afterward, Amy grinned slyly and said, "Am I a ten, Bill?" and Bill said, "No, well, I'd say about a four."

On the way over to Eddie's we drove by a place called Cherry Hill. The name wasn't really Cherry Hill, but that was what almost everybody called it, because the thing was mainly famous for what the boys called "cherry pickin'." Cherry Hill was a housing development that had never come into being. All it was was a smooth blacktop access road with a couple of culs-de-sac branching off it. There weren't any houses on those culs-de-sac, at least not yet, so a lot of the kids used them as places to park and neck. Amy and Bill never, ever went to Cherry Hill to park, but every once in a while, they said, they liked to cruise by and give the parkers a hard time. This seemed to be a popular sport, at least among those not fortunate enough to be equipped with parkable lovers. (The rich get richer and the poor get even.)

Amy turned off the main road, cut her headlights, and crept along through the dark at about five miles an hour. The muffler rumbled discreetly. Amy pulled into the first cul-de-sac and eased up behind its sole occupant, a white Camaro parked at the curb.

"Just watch this, Dave," Bill said. We were giggling nervously. Amy leaned on the horn, waited a second, and threw on the high beams. The Camaro was brilliantly illuminated. But nothing else happened. We had been hoping that somebody's big bare ass would wallow up out of the darkness, something Bill said happened all the time. "Once," he said, "this guy came hoppin' out of the car with his pants undone." But tonight there was no show. If the Camaro was occupied, the lovers in it were either oblivious or too frightened to move. After a couple of seconds, Amy threw it in reverse and drove away like hell.

Eddie Lober's house was in a relatively fashionable section of Bingham. Mr. Lober was a businessman of local importance, and his house was big. When we drove up, the front door was sinisterly unlit, but there were a dozen cars parked in front and we could hear music coming from inside. Two boys were peeing casually into the bushes. We passed them without comment and went inside.

The first thing to do was look for Greg Liszk, the boy who was going to drink the case of beer and make everybody rich. I had decided not to join the bet, but Bill had put up twenty dollars, which was a lot of money for him. Scott and Eric had each bet twenty-five.

"We're gonna be so rich I can almost taste it," Eric said.

We found Greg in the kitchen, where most of the party had gravitated, presumably in order to be closer to the beer. The keg was sitting in the middle of the floor and leaking foam onto the linoleum. Several hours of pedestrian traffic had turned the foam into a very fertile-looking mud. There were bloated cigarette butts floating everywhere. Greg was sitting on the counter near the sink, drinking beer out of a paper cup. His eyes were very red.

"He chickened out," somebody whispered to Bill.

"It was just too good to be true," Bill said.

Amy shook her head. "You guys are *terrible*." She and Mary wandered off. Frank Ellis, who had been keeper of the original "contract" with Greg, came over to explain.

"He says it was all a big joke," Frank said. "We had a case of St. Pauli Girl and everything. It cost damn near twenty bucks, the cocksucker. Joe tried to get him to pay up, anyway, but Liszk said he'd fight anybody who tried to come near him."

"We shoulda guessed, I guess," Bill said.

"You want some money for the beer?" Eric asked.

"Naw," Frank said. "We sold it to some sophomores for thirty."

I went into the living room and ran into Les Zulinski, who was just leaving.

"You missed divorce court," he said.

"What?"

He pointed over his shoulder. Cathy Logan, Mark Lobrano's true lover and lockermate, was dancing with some guy I'd never seen before. She did not look happy.

"There was this big fight," Les said. "I don't know what about. But Mark, man, he was fucking out of his mind. I thought he was going to bust the place up."

"Did he do that?" I said, pointing to a broken lamp whose ceramic base lay in a zillion pieces on the floor.

"Naw," Les said. "That was somebody else. All Mark did was bust a glass in the kitchen. I don't think he's even here anymore." Les said good-bye and took off.

Bill came out of the kitchen with two beers. He handed one to me.

"I got this for Amy," he said, "but you're here and she's not, so you win."

"Thanks."

The party certainly didn't look like much at this point. Cathy

Logan and the mystery man were the only people dancing. A couple of kids were sitting on the couch and sharing a joint. Across the room a sad-eyed fat girl sprawled in a chair. The music on the record player was the new Pink Floyd album, which contained one of Bill's favorite lyrics, "We don't need no education." I remembered listening to Pink Floyd ten years before, when the band's albums were cherished mainly as Muzak for LSD trips.

Eddie Lober wandered into the room, looking like a condemned man. He looked, in fact, as though he had been crying.

"The goddamned bathroom smells like puke," he said.

"The bathrooms at these parties *always* smell like puke," Bill whispered.

Eddie came over to where we were standing. "Jesus Christ," he said. "Somebody swiped a whole bottle of pills out of the kitchen." His face was ashen. "They were pills to make the fucking *cat* go to the *bathroom*." He moaned and walked away.

"Shit, man," Bill said. "I'm glad this isn't my house."

"Me, too."

"I think I better go look for Amy."

"See you later."

I went back into the kitchen. There wasn't really anybody there I knew, so I leaned against the counter and sipped my beer. Two boys I didn't recognize were talking about music.

"I don't like all them rock bands," one said. "Foreigner and Boston and like that. They all blow. They ain't original or nothin'."

"Asshole Lorenzo wanted the band to do some Foreigner stuff, but I said no way."

"You guys still together?"

"Yeah, man. We're jammin' over at Eisenhower next week."

"Is that guy Santo still the singer?"

"Naw, we booted him. He couldn't sing worth a shit."

"You guys do any Zep?"

"Yeah. About eighty percent."

"What else?"

"Song by Rush. Some Hendrix. Three new songs. One Deep Purple."

"You know Joe Mead is goin' around sayin' he's a better bass player than you?"

"Yeah. I seen him over at Burger King. I said, 'So, I hear you says you're better than me.' He says, 'I never did nothin' like that, no way.' And I says, 'Like shit.' And he says, 'I never said I was a better bass player than you.' And I says, 'Well you ain't. I heard you play. And you suck.'"

"That guy's a total asshole."

"Anyway, if he's better than I am, how come he ain't in the band?"

"Yeah."

"You still workin' at the roller rink?"

"Yeah."

"What's it like?"

"It's pretty decent. I gotta wear this fuckin' green uniform and skate around tellin' people to slow down and shit, but it's okay. Sometimes I work the counter handing out skates."

"You work every night?"

"Naw, just three a week. Thursday is rock night, but all the rest are disco."

"Disco?"

"Yeah. It blows."

"I didn't know they had disco at roller rinks."

"Yeah. All them guys that change the records are faggots, man. One of them came up for some skates and said, 'Thay, can I have some of them pretty yellow ones, please?' All the guys throw pennies at the record booth, tryin' to knock off the tone arm. It's a goof. When they hit the record, man, it's a total goof. It's a good job, though. Real easy. You don't have to do nothin'."

"Are you a bouncer?"

"Naw, they got two guys who weigh about six hundred pounds to do that. Nobody fucks with them."

I refilled my glass and bummed a cigarette. A couple of guys from the swimming team came in. Like most of the guys on the team, they had shaved their heads. Their "zip cuts," as they called them, were supposed to eliminate friction in the water and improve team spirit. One of the guys on the team, Bob Jonas, had even tried to talk me into having my head shaved. "But I'm not on the team," I said. "It don't matter," Bob assured me. "Anybody can do it." At that point only three or four guys had done it, and Bob was feeling lonely. Somebody asked Bob what his mother thought of his haircut. "She hates it," he said. "She told me, 'Every time I look at you all I can think of is *One Flew Over the Cuckoo's Nest.*'"

Most of the girls didn't like the zip cuts, either. I was told that the girl friend of one of the swimmers had taken one look at his head and handed him back his high school ring, but the story may have been exaggerated. Even so, the girls were justified in being upset. The boys had unsexed themselves for their sport, and all those bald heads were an ugly reminder that for the time being swimming came first and girls came second. "If your girl doesn't like your haircut," my old football coach used to tell us, "then you'd better find yourself a new girl." Coaches demand a sexual allegiance from their athletes that doesn't always leave much room for girl friends. Fortunately for the girls, the boys on the swimming team had been more restrained than the boys on the football team at a high school in a nearby town. The football players had all had their hair cut very short and then shaved their numerals on the sides of their heads.

The girls weren't doing too well at the party, either. At least, there weren't very many of them. And most of the ones I saw looked dejected. There were only two in the kitchen. They were standing by the refrigerator with their arms crossed, looking mean. They were both in my accounting class.

Scott wandered into the kitchen.

"You want a piece of gum?" he asked me.

"Sure."

"Here." He took the piece he was chewing out of his mouth and held it out to me, poker-faced.

"Very funny."

"This party blows, don't it?" Scott said, still holding his gum in his hand.

"Yup."

"Does it blow in here as much as it blows in the living room?"

"Just about even."

"That's what I figured. Seen Bill?"

"Nope."

"Me either."

Carl Morgan skimmed across the floor-mud, a beer in either hand, and paused briefly to say hello.

"You look really wasted," Scott said, flatteringly.

The two girls by the refrigerator were finally talking.

"I paid fifty dollars to have a phone installed in my room," one of them said, "and the fucker [her stepfather, a notorious madman] ripped it out of the wall. He said he didn't want to pay no more phone bills, even though I paid for it myself."

"I live with my grandparents now," the other one said. "They treat me all right. They're a goof."

"I tried to have the fucker arrested once, but they said they couldn't do it. So I gave him a six-pack for his birthday."

Scott got another beer and wandered away. I decided it was time for me to leave, but first I had to figure out where Bill and Amy were. When I finally found them they were standing in the darkest corner of the living room, necking. I realized I had never seen them kiss before (they didn't do it at school). Maybe this was their first time. After two or three minutes of waving at Bill, I finally caught his eye, waved good-bye, and bummed a ride home with a friend of Eric's, who was also taking him. On my way out the door I heard someone in the kitchen shouting, "Get out of here, Mimi, goddammit, you're just a sophomore, you homo."

Have high school parties ever been different? There were more drugs (and fewer kegs) at the ones I used to go to, but the end result was usually the same. I shudder to think of all the bathrooms I have thrown up in, propped against a toilet bowl, forgotten about until someone else barged in to vomit, or urinate in the sink. Parties in *junior* high school had a sounder rationale: You went to those to make out, or think about making out, or watch other people making out or thinking about making out. There was liquor sometimes, or marijuana, but never very much (it was hard to come by then), and the threat of parents, inevitably upstairs, kept things from getting too far out of hand. Besides, given the choice, who wouldn't prefer to *kiss*?

High school parties, on the other hand, are grotesque imitations of cocktail parties. Sex, by high school, is too far advanced to be party entertainment, except by accident (all those "mistakenly" opened bedroom doors). "Social drinking" is still a skill undreamed of ("Would you like a beer, or a glass of vodka?"). At one party I went to in tenth grade, everyone drank a beverage consisting of one-third beer, one-third vodka, and one-third Seven-Up. It was supposed to taste "exactly like beer." I knew a girl who drank nothing but Scotch and Dr. Pepper. Sobering thought. Why on earth, I found myself wondering as Eric's friend drove us home, rebounding happily from curb to curb at a hundred or so miles an hour, had I ever wanted to go back?

22
The Shit Hits the Fan

Mrs. Griswold taught a course in remedial English that met fourth period, just before my journalism class. One day remedial English lasted a little longer than usual, and one of the kids in it, a black girl, was talking with Mrs. Griswold when we arrived for journalism. On the blackboard were some sentences the remedial kids had been working on. Bill read one of them aloud in a mocking voice: "The dog has its collar." Several of the journalism kids laughed. The black girl was hurt and embarrassed. "What's the matter?" she said. "Is that too easy for you geniuses?" Mrs. Griswold bit her tongue. When the black girl left, she lashed into us.

"Oh, that's just great," she shouted. "That's just terrific. You see I'm trying to help somebody and you shoot off your big mouth and make her feel terrible. Did you see the look on that girl's face? And Bill Scalet, of all people. Half the kids in remedial spell better than you do. I'm sick of this superior attitude. I'm sick of all this fooling around. If you don't exert a little self-control—and I mean all of you—then you are going to find yourselves in some very serious trouble. I'm *sick* of it."

Bill tried to laugh it off, but it was clear that he felt bad about what he had done. "I really didn't see her," he said quietly to no one in particular. "I really didn't see her." He kept quiet for the rest of the period. By lunchtime he was feeling himself again. He said, "All the colored guys just walk around saying, 'What you call me?' 'Huh?' 'What you call me?' 'Huh?' 'What you call me?' 'Huh?'"

Things were not going very well for Bill in journalism at the moment. Amy's moderating influence had begun to wear off, and lately he had been more rambunctious than usual. His temporary truce with the cheerleaders had ended, and so had his participation in most of the day-to-day workings of the newspaper. I think he was beginning to get nervous about his impending graduation. He never talked about it, but I could tell he was preoccupied. He had no article assignment for the next issue, the third, and he spent most of his time in class working on phony handouts of one sort or another. One day he holed up in the Publications Office writing notes to every member of the staff. "Dear Mr. Owen," mine began,

> *I am afraid you have not been working very hard
> in journalism and your spending too much time with
> that scoundril Bill Scalet and his friends. They are
> trouble makers and they have a very bad influence
> on you. Your article on guidance sucked. I am sorry
> to say it but it was the worst thing we have ever
> printed in this newspaper including Linda Smoleys
> Fashion roundup. As a result of your badness I am
> moving you onto the yearbook where you belong.*
> > *Sincerely,*
> > *Mrs. Griswold.*

Most of the kids thought the notes were pretty funny, but one of the cheerleaders, Vikki Anderson, showed hers to Mrs.

Griswold. She didn't mention it in class the next day, but she did ask Bill to meet with her after school. Scott and I hung around in front of the building to wait for him.

"She didn't yell at me or nothin'," Bill said as we walked along. "She just told me that if I did it again she'd nail my ass."

"What a bitch," Scott said.

We walked in silence for a while. Bill was brooding.

"I'm gonna get that cunt," he said finally.

"Which one?" Scott asked.

"That fucking Vikki Anderson. That fucking little fat cheerleading cunt." We went into the little grocery store at the center of town to buy Cokes and candy bars, then went our separate ways.

The next morning Bill came over to my locker. "Get a load of this," he said. He opened his notebook. Inside was a phony press release consisting of a crude caricature of Vikki with a paragraph of text beneath it.

"I'm a regular Michelangelo, ain't I?" Bill said.

The girl in the picture was sitting at a table covered with food. The text read:

FAT SOPHOMORE GIRL EATS TRIPLES

News Flash::::: Vikki Anderson became the first person to successfully eat three hot lunches at one setting. Vikkis meal was 8 cheese burgers, 2 plates of spagetty, 3 donuts, 1 chocalate pudding, with an apple in her mouth like a pig. Also she drank 43 cartons of chocalate milk and a box of ice cream sandwiches. Bingham students know Vikki by her fat -ss which can be clearly seen in her cherleader suit on Fridays. She ways 400 pounds and is 4 feet tall. Other students are occasionally crushed to death when she walks past them in the hall. Vikkis only friend Sheila McNichols said "I like her but I swear she is a fat pig."

"Me and Scott are gonna make about a million copies," Bill said, "and then put one in every locker. Want in?"

"Not really," I said. "Anyhow, I don't have journalism today."

"Shit." He thought for a moment. "Anyway, it's gonna be tough. Just wait and see."

I didn't hear anything more about it until that afternoon, when Carl Morgan stopped me in the hall. "You hear what happened?" he said.

"No."

"Griswold fired Bill as coeditor."

"No shit?"

"Honest to God. He got sent down to Shenck and everything."

"Was it the press release?"

"Yeah, man; the cheerleaders went through his notebook when he was out of the room and put one of those things on Griswold's desk. The shit really hit the fan, man."

I didn't run into Bill until after school. He was fairly chipper.

"You shoulda been there, man," he told me. "Shenck went out of his fucking mind. Said he'd never seen anything so juvenile in his whole career. And Griswold made me not an editor anymore. I'm just a regular staff guy now. Which is okay with me, to tell you the truth, because it's sure gonna make things easier. She said I wasn't mature enough to handle the responsibility."

"That's tough," I said.

"Aw, it's not so bad. And the way I figure it, I'm in so much trouble in that place now that it really doesn't matter if I get in a little more. I've been thinking, like, when Mrs. Griswold asks me if I've finished my article, I'll say, 'What's a matter, Griswold, ya got a bug up yer ass?' and stuff like that."

I laughed.

"Oh, yeah, one day she says to me, 'Why do you have to tell so many jokes and disrupt everything?' I wanted to tell her, 'Auuugh, Mrs. Griswold, I've just got all these jokes in my head.'" He squeezed his temples with both hands. "'I'll *try* to get them out, I'll *try* to get them out.'" He rolled his head around and made a sound like a tape recorder playing in reverse.

"I don't know, man," he said after a moment. "Sometimes I get so upset about things. I mean, things that are happening in the world, the stuff you see on TV, the stuff Mr. Bartlett yaps about. And I think, hey, people should know about this stuff—like the boat people, you know?—but then I think, why bother. Nobody has a sense of humor. Something always trips me up. If it isn't Griswold, it's the cheerleaders, and if it isn't the cheerleaders, it's somebody else. It just isn't worth all the trouble."

When all the fuss about the press release had died down, Bill became calmer and more relaxed than I had seen him all semester. He even started to work on an article for the next issue.

I, meanwhile, had decided to leave Bingham High. It was still a couple of weeks till the end of the term, but I was beginning to tire of my schedule. More important, Ann was beginning to loathe it. Our weeknight social life had tapered off to nothing, and lately I had been going to Bingham on weekends, too. My high school life was simply beginning to seem too natural to me; for more than three months it had *been* my life. I had been hoping to go to the Winter Cotillion (Susan Mattey had asked me, vaguely; I told her I was already going), but I knew I could never get Ann to go with me, and in the end I decided that one high school dance was more than enough. Furthermore, Ann and I were planning to go out of town for Christmas, and I needed some free time beforehand. I let a few more days go by and then began to drop hints.

"You still don't have an article for this issue," Mrs. Griswold told me one day. "Do you want one?"

"I don't know," I said. "I got this personal situation at home."

"Do you want to talk about it?"

"Oh, it's nothing like that," I said. "It's just that my dad got a new job and we may all be moving again."

"What do you think about that?"

"Oh, I don't mind. It's kind of fun moving around."

"Do you know where you're going to go?"

"Yeah. California."

"Well, that'll be exciting, anyway. Too bad it's senior year."

Mrs. Griswold was very kind. We talked for ten or fifteen minutes more. She never pressed for details, but she wanted to make sure that I was happy with the move. I think that if I had told her I didn't want to go, she would have talked to my parents or the principal and tried to work something out. I was genuinely touched, all the more so because by that point I was feeling so comfortable in my adopted role that I almost believed I was really going to California.

I told Bill that same day in the Publications Office.

"You're fucking kidding," he said.

"Naw, it's a pretty sure thing. We might even go next week."

"What a bummer. You should try to do something about it. They shouldn't be able to push you around like that."

"Oh, I don't know," I said. "It could be decent."

"But man, you won't *know* anybody."

"I didn't know anybody when I came here. But I still had a good time. And I've never been to California."

"Where in California are you moving?" Scott asked.

"Near San Francisco someplace."

"Oh, Jesus," Bill said. "It's completely homo out there. Fifty fucking percent of the people are faggots." We had a long debate about whether I would turn into a homo.

"I'll watch myself," I said finally.

At lunch that day I was late getting my tray, and by the time I spotted Bill, Scott, Eric, and the other guys, there was only one place left at their table. Another boy from journalism got to it before I did, so I went over to an empty table and sat alone. But just as I started to eat, I heard Bill calling me. He waved me over. He and the other guys, it turned out, had told the boy from journalism that the seat was taken. They had been saving it for me. And that, I think, was the high point of my semester.

23
&Leaving

      I met with Julia a few days later and we worked out a plan for getting me out of school. Since the administration thought I was a legitimate student, I couldn't simply disappear. The last thing we wanted was for a truant officer to go nosing around Bingham trying to find me. We decided that I would pretend to be sick for a few days, and then Julia would call in to explain that we were moving away. Julia would have to write a letter to the school, but since I was old enough to drop out, there shouldn't be any complications.

    Before I could leave, however, there was one thing I had to do: play in the final volleyball game of the season. We had begun playing volleyball in gym when the weather turned cool in November. Mr. Meiden divided our section of the class into four teams and set up a round-robin tournament covering a period of about six weeks. I was on a team with Les, Frank Beauchamp, Jennifer Hughes, and another girl, who had joined the class halfway through the term. When the tournament ended our team was tied for first place. I had intended to make the following day, a Friday, my final day at Bingham, but now a playoff match was scheduled for Tuesday. Ann's father was coming to New York that day and we were supposed to meet him in the afternoon. If I put in a full day at school, I'd never be able to get home in time. I considered skipping the game altogether, but I felt bad about missing the championship match. It wasn't that my services as a volleyball player would have been missed; they certainly wouldn't have been. But I felt bad about walking out on the team, which was small enough as it was. I also wanted to play in the game; gym had continued to be one of my favorite activities, and it was fun to be on a winning team. In the end I decided that if I left school immediately after the game, at noon, I could just make it back in time. So I had Ann forge me a note saying I had a doctor's appointment at 12:30, and I reserved a taxicab to take me to a nearby town where I could catch an early bus to New York.

The day of the game did not begin auspiciously. I got to town late and ran all the way to school so I wouldn't be late for homeroom. The traffic on the main road, which I had to cross, was heavy, and as I ran I kept looking over my shoulder for a break in the flow. When I turned to run for an opening, I ran straight into a tree. A big branch caught me across the bridge of the nose and knocked both lenses out of my glasses. I felt as though I'd been hit in the head with a baseball bat. I spent most of first period in the nurse's office having little pieces of bark picked out of my skin. The throbbing in my head made the rest of the day feel distinctly unreal. I could almost believe that my leaving Bingham was causing some eerie transformation in my brain.

By the time gym rolled around, my nose had stopped bleeding and I had managed to get the lenses back in my glasses. I still had a headache, and an ugly wound on the bridge of my nose, but I was in reasonably good shape. Les and Frank were excited about the game.

"We're gonna murder the mothers," Les said as we got dressed. "You been practicing your serve?"

"Yeah," I said. My serve had given us some problems early in the tournament. In our first game I think I only managed to get one serve over the net. Once I missed the ball completely, a stunning display of athletic incompetence that triggered not gales but hurricanes of laughter in the class. "I don't think I've ever seen anyone do that before," Mr. Meiden said. I was very embarrassed. And I couldn't figure out what was wrong. I had never had any trouble serving volleyballs in all the years I had played the game in school and on picnics. But now I couldn't even connect with the ball. I would hold it in my left hand, bring my right fist up carefully to meet it, and make a spectacle of myself. I was in a panic. I spent more than an hour that night hitting a knotted towel around our apartment. Ann wondered if I had lost my mind. My practice session didn't end until I had knocked over and destroyed a little glass carousel that Ann had had since she was twelve.

I finally decided that my problem was the result of an old injury. Two years before, I had broken my right wrist severely in a long fall, and I had never quite regained full mobility. I decided that the fracture must have thrown off my already marginal coordination. That's what I told myself, anyway. In the next game I did all my serving with my left hand, and the problem disappeared. I later switched to a right-handed, over-hand serve, which also worked fine. But to this day I am unable to make an underhand volleyball serve with my right hand.

Despite my deficiencies as a server, our team did very well. Les and Frank were both expert players, and together they carried the team. I was considerably less skillful than either of them, but I was better than both of the girls, so I figured that I was, at worst, a neutral factor on the team. My single asset was that I was a couple of inches taller than either Les or Frank and therefore of some value at the net. Possibly in an attempt to bolster my damaged pride, Les began calling me "Spike," a nickname that might have stuck if I had stayed at Bingham longer: By the time I dropped out, there were six or seven kids who called me nothing but that.

The play-off game, unfortunately, did not go well, but I was glad I had decided to take part. We matched the other team point for point through the first half of the game, dropped behind for a little while, and then came back to lose by a nose. The play-off game was the only activity scheduled for the day, so all the other kids in the class sat in the bleachers and watched. Luckily for me, my serve only let me down once. That's the sort of lapse that could happen to anyone, I told myself, but since I had a history of screwing up, Les made sure I understood it was not to happen again.

After the game I showed my note to Mr. Meiden and left the gym before the other kids went to lunch. I had decided not to tell Les and Frank that I was leaving, thinking that the fewer people who knew about it the less likely it would be that any of them would try to track me down. A week would pass before anyone thought it odd that I was no longer in school, and then Christmas vacation would begin. By the time it ended, no one would remember or care.

I opened my locker for the last time, gathered up my notebook, my coat, and a few odd socks, and made sure all my textbooks were inside, so someone could collect them later. I went down to the Publications Office to see if any of the kids were there, but they were all in the classroom working on assignments. I spotted Bill through the window in the door, but couldn't catch his eye. I took the long way out, down the rear upper corridor and the back stairs, and headed for a side entrance. At the door I ran into three or four girls I knew, including Susan Mattey.

"Sneaking out?" she said.

"Not exactly. I've gotta go to the doctor."

"What did you do to your nose?" one of the other girls asked.

"I ran into a tree."

"What?"

"I mean I got into a fight with some thugs who were trying to throttle an old lady."

"That's better," Susan said.

"And every word of it's true."

"I bet."

"Well, see you later."

"Yeah, see ya."

"Bye."

"Bye."

And so I left. I cut across the empty lot beside the school, turned down the main drag, passed a couple of kids on their way back from an illicit lunch at the candy counter of the drugstore, and only looked back once.

℘Afterword:
My Class

In 1968, when Bill Scalet and most of the other members of my class were six years old, Theodore Roszak wrote that young people were almost singlehandedly responsible for "most of what is presently happening that is new, provocative, and engaging in politics, education, the arts, [and] social relations (love, courtship, family, community)." Roszak isn't always a very reliable observer of American culture, but what is important is that a dozen years ago it was possible for anyone to say such things. Roszak even went further, claiming that "the alienated young are giving shape to something that looks like the saving vision our endangered civilization requires."

No one is saying anything like that now, of course. When social commentators talk about young people today, the themes are a bit less exhilarating—things like draft registration, deteriorating schools, declining SATs, rising tuitions, soaring unemployment, diminishing opportunities. For a kid just about to be turned loose on the world, all that rising, soaring, declining, and deteriorating adds up to a pretty unsettling picture. Bill and his friends are going to have to learn to get along in a world that doesn't expect very much of them.

Nor has that world given them as much as it might have. Ordinarily I think there are few people more tedious than those who complain about the inadequacies of contemporary education. The students don't know this, the students don't know that. High school teachers are fallible human beings who work too hard for too little money in communities that are too often ungrateful.

But as the weeks and months went by I found myself getting angrier and angrier about the ignorance that was not only condoned but even cultivated at Bingham High. In the simplest, most fundamental sense, the majority of my classmates were not being educated. The situation is unlikely to improve. Tales of woe about the shortcomings of our schools have made the problems self-perpetuating. Statistics have absolved the teachers of responsibility. More than one of my teachers explained his rationale for not assigning papers by saying, "The kids don't know how to write." Mr. Quennell once told us before a test, "Try to write in complete sentences," but he didn't make a fuss when we didn't. He never corrected the grammar in our tests, never noted misspellings on anything but vocabulary quizzes, never pointed out a sentence fragment or a pronoun that didn't have an antecedent or a comma that should have been a period. When students in my history class had trouble writing even the brief essays that Mr. Bartlett's tests required, they were encouraged to write their answers in outline form. "This isn't English class," Mr. Bartlett said. When students in my accounting class had trouble adding up figures on ledger sheets, they were issued pocket calculators. "This isn't math class," Mrs. Medina said. Mr. Quennell once told us, "I used to assign *two papers a semester* in this class. You kids don't know how lucky you are."

The lucky members of my class don't know how to make a

sentence or a paragraph, and they balk at adding half a dozen three-digit numbers. Never mind that they don't know Latin, or French, or chemistry, or biology, or algebra, or European history; they've been cheated out of skills so fundamental it's hard to imagine them getting along from one day to the next.

Even so, the kids I knew at Bingham were almost without exception optimistic about their futures and, somewhat less emphatically, about the future of their country. Most of the kids I met expected to own bigger houses and better cars than their parents did, and they were certain they would make more money—lots more. They believed the gas shortage was illusory, that scientists would solve the energy crisis by inventing an inexhaustible source of inexpensive energy, that the American economy was suffering temporary difficulties that would take care of themselves in a year or two.

The members of my class who go to college will graduate in 1984, the year we like to pretend will seal our doom. I hope they won't be disappointed in the world they inherit. If they are, I hope that by then they will have learned enough, one way or another, to do something about it.

I may be silly to worry about my classmates. It is extremely difficult, after all, to look at a teenager and predict what he or she will become. A high school is a world of its own, with its own codes of conduct and its own rules of survival. That is one of the reasons why "senior prophecies" so often turn out to be laughably wrong: Success or failure—socially, academically, athletically—in a high school does not necessarily have much to do with success or failure in the world beyond it. High school reunions, much more than their college counterparts, tend to be full of surprises. The powerful editor of the newspaper turns out to have become a third-rate real-estate salesman, the homecoming queen is a lonely spinster without any friends, the least popular kid in the class runs an international corporation and is the life of parties all over the world. If I ever go back to a Bingham reunion, I may find a roomful of strangers.

Although I don't envy their futures, I feel grateful to have shared my classmates' lives for a few months. How often one wishes one could somehow be transported back to adolescence for a little while, to say things now irretrievably unsaid, or to cross out a few unfortunate lines in a literary magazine. If only it were possible to go back and do it all differently. I've had a chance to do that, in a small way. And now that it's over—now that I have to sit back and think of all the things I did or forgot to do at Bingham, and all the stupid things I said—I catch myself cringing a little and thinking, If only . . .

Author's Note

Asked to define the word "faction" one day in Mr. Bartlett's class, Bill Scalet guessed "a cross between fact and fiction." That, I suppose, is an acceptable description of this book. In order to disguise the school I attended, its location, its students, and its teachers, I have changed all names and mixed identities. Since a high school isn't a restaurant or a farmhouse filled with antiques, I can't imagine that any reader would ever try to track this one down. If for some reason someone should, the "hints" scattered throughout the text will prove unhelpful, since I have changed them, too.

Because virtually none of my former classmates read any books whatsoever outside of school, I doubt that any of them will stumble across this one. Even if they do, they will have trouble finding themselves in it. None will discover himself intact; few will be able to recognize even pieces of themselves with absolute certainty. The identifications they may make will be of the sort that any reader makes with the characters of a book. As for the small handful of my close friends who think they know where I went every day, I must admit that I have deceived them, too. My wife is in on the secret, of course, but unless I ask her to go to the prom, she'll keep it to herself.